Praise for Toby Marshall's Previous Books

"This book will have a major impact on the bottom line of organisations."

Eve Crestani,
Company Director and Business Consultant

"Frank, often entertaining and extremely practical – absolute gold! This is an excellent resource without the ego – well worth a read."

Lesley Horsburgh,
Managing Editor of 'Recruitment EXTRA'

"Useful advice – not the usual bulldust!"
(last word in this quote required editing)

Annie de Botton,
HR Manager Wealth and Asset Management, Perpetual

"Easy to read, practical advice."

Melanie Laing,
Asia Pacific Director HR, Unisys

"A good racy read with lots of valuable insights."

Warwick James,
Managing Director of Warwick James & Partners

"Innovative and insightful – a great resource for up and coming professionals to boost their career."

Tim Dein,
President NSW AHRI Council (Australian Human Resources Institute)

"A refreshingly candid account...results in some powerful insights. A must read for anyone and everyone involved in business today."

Elinor Crossing,
Talent Management Consultant

D1367286

© www.leadcreation.com.au

Praise for Toby Marshall's Work

"Toby has revolutionised my thinking around marketing and the electronic media. We attended a meeting and workshop yesterday which were filled with new ideas and 'invaluable' sharing of the results of his research. The intellectual property he has created around the use of LinkedIn to broaden the recognition of our services and brand is cutting edge. Absolutely first class communicator who can translate the jargon into knowledge bites I can understand. We are looking forward to the journey, thanks Toby."

Francois Paquette,
Principal at Dean Kavanagh Advisory Services

"Like many businesses, we had a great product but not enough people knew about it. That's why we went to **lead creation**—and they had a huge impact on our business. We worked with Toby Marshall and **lead creation** in mid 2008 when the GFC was starting and even during this appalling market managed to achieve a sales growth of 32%. We've had even better results in our much bigger UK market. The **lead creation** strategies are simple but effective for businesses with a good product who just need more prospects to hear about it. And the best part was, I didn't have to go on the road and do any hard selling! The **lead creation** system really works to bring in qualified leads for my company."

Paul Resnik
Consultant to the Australian and global Financial Advisory Industry

"Toby is one of the most honorable, sincere, committed and innovative businesspeople I have encountered in a ridiculously long life. I have learnt a great deal from him and been inspired by his energy and commitment. I have never known him to be less than delightful company and he has always lifted my spirits."

John J. Howard,
Owner Arkouda Associates

See the back of the book for more testimonials!

Toby Marshall

Small Business Internet Marketing

Ideas & Solution for Advertising Small Businesses Online : The Sales Lead Generation Bible

"Small business marketing is my passion — delivering qualified new clients to small businesses. My company lead creation tailors the power of internet marketing and direct response marketing to the very different needs of small and micro business. Advertising small businesses in an innovative way is what we do."

- **Toby Marshall**

"Recently, I attended a seminar which Toby ran. It was fabulous! Toby provided us with a wealth of information in a short time-frame & I came away with plenty of ideas to implement. I would have no hesitation in recommending Toby for anyone needing help in generating leads."

Debbie Carr,
Director of True Colours Recruitment

Thanks to the Team

This is a wide ranging book which covers all aspects of small business marketing. Numerous young staff and interns contributed their expertise and hard work to make this in-depth book possible. A big thank you for all your help and passion.

Chief editor and writing coordinator: Melanie Wagner
The team:

- Carli Alman – Copywriter
- Vahe Arabian – SEO
- Alyse Cassaniti – Administration
- Lauren Diver-Tuck – Copywriter
- Emilie Donnell – Administration & Editing
- Valentine Gunadharma – Designer
- Louise Hardy – Copywriter
- Daryl Kong – Social Networking/LinkedIn specialist
- Joe Lam – Google AdWords
- Chia Lee Tai – Web Design
- Amanda Liu – Administration & Editing
- Caroline Maroon – HR
- Rosalie Odtojan – PR
- Melissa Pham – Administration
- Samantha Rego – HR & Administration
- Jani Senevirante – Copywriter
- Lincoln Smith – IT, SEO & AdWords
- Elizabeth Somerville – Copywriter
- Wendy Trieu – Web Design
- Mai Vo – Google AdWords
- Melanie Wagner – Head Copywriter
- Carla Wainer – Social Networking
- Sarah Wooltorton - Copywriter
- Katrina Wong – Social Networking/Twitter Specialist

Learn more about us at http://www.leadcreation.com.au/our-team

Contents

Chapter 1: Small Business Marketing—Getting More Customers with Cost-Effective and Hassle-Free Marketing

The Best Marketing Advice You'll Ever Get.

Let's start this marketing journey by cutting to the chase. By being really blunt:

> Small Business[1] Marketing is **only** about getting more customers—about generating leads that become the sort of clients you want many more of.
>
> Everything else like 'raising your profile' is just so much hot air. Or falls in the category of "nice to have, but way too expensive for my small business".

This famous quote from John Wanamaker sums up the advertising and marketing dilemma of <u>big</u> business:

> "Half the money I spend on advertising is wasted;
> the trouble is I don't know which half."

Well, you'll soon discover that in advertising <u>small</u> businesses, the wastage is typically 80%, and we <u>**do**</u> know where most of it is wasted.

---

[1] What is small business? It's companies with sales of under $10 million a year, employing less than a hundred staff. Right down to a solopreneur working from home.

Where is the 80% wasted by small business?

Well, my mate Bob[2] runs a small business in Melbourne and what he went through perfectly illustrates the incredible wastage that can occur when an SME starts a marketing journey.

Bob provides financial advice to very wealthy families, his office is in the rich inner Melbourne suburb of Toorak. His team of five professionals provide a great service, and it's a very profitable business.

One morning in February 2008 Bob arrived in the office and surprised his staff by saying he was a bit tired of being the main salesperson. That since he was bored with constantly going out and doing presentations and running seminars, he thought he'd invest in some marketing to get some new clients instead.

Turns out a few sales people had been to see him—hard selling people whose message had fallen on receptive ears.

The first was a consultant selling 'Position and Brand your Business'. And $8,000 later, Bob had a new logo and a new letterhead. Plus he had a 'strategy' to raise the profile of his new brand. It didn't worry Bob that most of this bloke's clients were large companies, for whom this sort of money was 'pocket change'. It didn't occur to him that it might be a problem.

The branding consultant then introduced the alarmingly attractive Brenda who sells advertising in an industry magazine, plus 'special'

---

[2] Name changed to protect the guilty! And for you non-Oz's, mate just means a friend. We're not married!

sponsorship rights to their conferences. Bob is like most men, and so $15,000 seemed like a great investment.

Then a species that hopefully small business will not encounter for too much longer turned up on the doorstep: a web designer. Young and stylish, he and his partner built great looking websites. $3000, plus $100 a month to host. Great deal, thought Bob.

The last salesman to knock on Bob's door seemed to offer the last piece of the puzzle: Qualified leads, delivered on a plate, using Google AdWords. "These prospects will see my new logo and new positioning statement, so it was a no—brainer" said Bob. Just $12,000 and leads will flow for 12 whole months. "One client will pay for it all!" said the salesman.

So, Bob had now spent $38,000, a large chunk of his net profit for the year. Plus ongoing monthly charges, some of which he was yet to become aware of (courtesy of the spiky haired web designers).

And he sat back and waited for the clients. And waited. He rang the salespeople and told them not much was happening. They told him he had 'raised his profile' and to be patient, that the clients would come. But Bob had now turned off the money flow and the advertisements weren't appearing anymore—and if his 'profile' had ever been raised, it was now sinking fast. In fact his 'profile' was following his money down the plughole.

Bob would probably still be hoping that some new clients would shortly appear if we hadn't had a chat the last time I was down in Melbourne. He was tearing the last of his hair out as he realised he'd been conned. He's now back on the road doing what he has done for twenty-three years, selling, while he slowly and cautiously considers buying *lead creation*'s marketing system. I appreciate he is a bit jaundiced about marketers and that it may take some time!

I'm unhappy as well, because he hadn't read this book and called us first—we build an entire marketing system for less than half of what he wasted. But at least one person was a winner: The young and incredibly attractive Brenda got a nice bonus!

Once you've read this book you'll know there were some _really_ important pieces missing from Bob's marketing strategy. Pieces that meant he had zero chance of getting a flow of leads – in Australia, we say he had Buckley's chance. Here are some of the main ones:

- **'SEO'** was MISSING: this is what enables people to actually find your website
- **Persuasion Copywriting** was MISSING: the words that people read or hear on your website must make them want to get to know you and to download your stuff
- **Autoresponder** was MISSING: this is the technology that automatically sends potential clients your great information.
- **User control** was MISSING: the autoresponder and website will need to be updated regularly—so you need to do it yourself, and not pay $500 every time to the spiky haired web designers!

You'll also discover as you read further why 'image' or 'profile raising' advertising in magazines, newspapers and radio is just a waste for a small business like Bob's. And finally, you'll see that charging that amount of money on Google AdWords for a micro business is just obscene. No other word for it. Less than $2,000 will generate customers for 95% of small businesses _if_ you follow the strategies in Chapter 8 on AdWords.

Advertising Small Business

Most small business owners wanting more clients take this phrase literally. And they go out and buy advertisements in the mass media—newspapers, magazines and radio. Which costs a fortune and has dubious benefits. Advertising small businesses means something very different in this book, as you'll discover. It means <u>promoting</u> your small business, and they are poles apart.

It means using one of a number of different techniques to get your message out to the people you want to read it. It means internet marketing; social networking; videos on YouTube; building a big profile on LinkedIn. And yes, god forbid, advertising your small business may find you on Twitter (where no-one wants to know what you had for lunch!).

Small Business Marketing that Actually WORKS.

If you are going to part with your hard earned money, any marketing you do must have ALL of the following components:

1. It needs to be diverse, you don't want to put all your eggs in one basket. Bob bought four extremely large (and overpriced) baskets, but he really needed nine smaller and more affordable ones.

2. All the components need to work together. Bob had Google AdWords, but no-one told him about Landing Pages—critical for small business marketing (Chapter 4: Persuasion Copywriting). Or Autoresponders (Chapter 7: Autoresponders). He had a website, but Spiky Hair didn't tell him about small business SEO (Chapter 3: Search Engine Optimization – Spiky's not too sure

about optimization anyway[3], let alone why it's different to what big companies do. But hey, he loves building cool websites.)

3. It needs to be measurable. Your results need to be quantifiable so you can see what's working and what's a dog. What's getting you good leads and sales and what isn't. So you then spend more on what works and maybe shoot the dog.

4. It needs to be testable <u>before</u> you spend big money (pretty hard to do with ads in Magazines!). For example: if you need five Google AdWords campaigns, build <u>one</u> on low traffic words and make sure everything works. Then test and tweak it on high traffic words. When it works, build the other 4 campaigns.

5. It needs to be 'off the shelf' where possible. So it's robust, scaleable and connectable. And someone else is worrying about making the technology work better as internet marketing changes at warp speed. Web sites and the technology to stay in touch with your clients are now virtually free. Something Spiky Hair is going to painfully have to live with. Maybe he'll move into SEO, just as that stops being flavor of the year!

Marketing that has these five components is called Direct Response Marketing. Before we look at this type of small business marketing in more detail, let's clear some misconceptions up...

---

[3] I once pointed out to a spiky that the truly beautiful $11,000 site he had just proudly shown me was now 6 months old but didn't appear in the first 500 Google results for their main keyword. The site was invisible online. His response: "SEO is a waste of money; it only works for a short time". Amazingly narrow sighted and WRONG!

© www.leadcreation.com.au

Small Business' Common Marketing Misconceptions

Misconception #1

"Sales is marketing". No. It's *sales*. And sales always involves people trying to talk to/talking to potential customers. Marketing, on the other hand, brings people into your 'funnel' so you can later sell to them <u>after</u> you are positioned as the expert. (More on this later.)

Misconception #2

That "the kind of marketing done by large companies is the same as what small businesses need to do". This is simply rubbish but believing it is destructive of your hard earned money. Almost equivalent to buying a yacht—just a hole that you pour money into which quickly vanishes!

For a large company, their advertising and marketing essentially focuses on building a brand, building their image in the marketplace. They do this because:

1. **It builds the profile and recall of their brand so people will more likely choose their products or services**
2. **It pleases the board of directors and senior management who like most people know little about marketing. But they sure have strong opinions, and have the clout to get their views heard**
3. **It wins awards for advertising which makes management feel good**
4. **And a distant fourth reason, because they want to sell something!**

The marketing department in big companies has a real battle on its hands if it wants to create marketing that is effective. Now, if it's hard for them, it's <u>impossible</u> for you. Brand marketing is very expensive which just makes it ridiculous for small businesses who don't have big budgets to blow on hit and miss campaigns. Or the money to spend on something as vague as 'raising their profile'.

Which brings us back to **Direct Response Marketing.** If you follow the strategies in this book, you'll see it is very effective, low-cost and simple to implement. Most importantly, a small business can quickly see what works and what doesn't – and then do more of what works.

Direct marketing was pioneered in the world of hard selling consumer junk marketing—weight loss, muscle building, Readers Digest, etc. So many small business owners who are professionals or sell BtoB are rightly skeptical. They believe it could make them look 'unprofessional' in the eyes of their industry colleagues.

Well they'd be right if they started selling their Accounting services alongside the cellulite ads on late night television. Or put their Risk Management services in the local newspaper alongside "Once only, never to be repeated offers" with giant headlines and semi-naked models!

The truth is that there are some very good principles that underlie these hard selling and crass advertisements. At *lead creation* we have spent nearly five years working with mentors and studying the techniques and how to adapt them to the world of small services businesses. And in particular, professional services marketing—which needs to be a long way away from the "you too can lose a hundred pounds in two weeks" ads!

What are some of the principles that can be adapted? We've already discussed a major one: the need to test before you waste your money. Brilliant.

However the main one is the need to start building a relationship slowly. Give something away that your audience values that doesn't cost you too much. Something that establishes your credibility. That does the 'Heavy Lifting' for your business <u>before</u> you get on the phone. So you can stay as the kindly Dr Jekyll and not switch to the hard selling Mr. Hyde, which rather ruins your positioning as the 'expert adviser' (and isn't that where we all need to be?).

As we've seen, Direct Response is ideal for a small business with a limited budget and lots of competitors. And using its proven techniques to acquire new Gold Clients <u>must</u> be the number one priority of small business marketing. It's <u>only</u> the opinions these clients have about your marketing that counts, not your competitors or the customers you don't want.

> **Your Gold Clients:** *The large niche of A-List clients who are the most profitable for <u>your</u> small business. A well-defined group to whom you provide high service levels for a premium price.*

Cost-effective marketing that gets these Gold Clients through your door is paramount. Once you provide them with a professional service, 'word of mouth' quickly becomes an important part of your marketing strategy. Gold Clients and their referrals will ensure the stability, profitability and growth of your small business into the future.

Direct Marketing Power: What It Can Do For You

Now you've got lots and lots of competitors like all SMEs. So how do you stand out? Well fundamentally, all those competitors are doing the same things—they are <u>selling</u> to their potential clients, and trying to do media advertising and fill seminar rooms. If you continue to do what they do, you can expect the same poor results they get. Your marketing strategy needs to make you stand out from the bunch and position you as the expert.

Direct Response Marketing is an extremely effective, low-cost and simple marketing strategy to implement in order to reach your Gold Clients and increase your profit margins. Direct Marketing contacts potential clients through mail, email, faxes, telemarketing, social networking and so on with the express purpose of prompting them to respond. For this reason, it is an incredibly effective and powerful way to market <u>when it is done correctly and professionally</u>. Each of these areas is a separate topic that we will cover in detail within this book.

How to Protect Your Small Business – The Importance of Marketing

If asked what business you are in, your initial answer might be, 'Financial Planning' or 'Business Coaching'. There are two other correct answers to this question, however, that are not often obvious to people working in professional services like Financial Advisory, coaching, the law, etc.

<u>Did you know that:</u>

Firstly, you are in <u>The Marketing Business</u>

While your initial answer is right – you generate your income by providing financial advice – this is a relatively lowly paid and relatively replaceable activity. Your *real money* instead comes from having <u>a system that generates new clients for your small business.</u> This business is a marketing business – whether it's business to business marketing or business to consumer marketing. Without a marketing system, you are limiting yourself in the recruitment of new clients and inhibiting the growth of your small business.

The far more challenging part of any small business is not providing your service but the marketing of that service. Once you make *that* your personal focus, then you are in the marketing business, and you can give yourself the best possible chance of ensuring your future and improving your profitability.

Secondly, you are in The Self-Aggrandisement Business

Now, this was a hard notion for a professional like me to accept, who was an accountant, then a marketing manager in investment banking and then a marketer in executive recruitment. To me my profession was accounting or marketing. So when I first heard the concept that *all* professionals are in the self-aggrandisement business, I thought: *What a load of rubbish.*

But clearly I thought about it some more.

Success is not always (some even say usually) about talent or intelligence. There are many very talented and very smart professionals who earn a lot less than a net of $250,000 per annum from their small business.

This is where Self-Aggrandisement comes in. If your clients believe *you* are the *only* person that can solve their problems they won't go to anyone else, and you can charge premium fees for your premium advice to that niche.

However, getting them to believe you are the 'only one' is a big ask unless you specialize in solving the problems of people like them. And you do it every day. So you really understand them. Of course, to make this level of specialization profitable, they must be a group worthy of such focused attention.

This leads you to the two key questions underlying this book:

1) Who are <u>your</u> gold clients?
2) How do you make them aware of your expertise and understanding of their specialist needs?

Who Are Your Gold Clients?

Gold Clients are simply the type of clients you need to run a highly profitable small business. They are identified by four factors – they are Reachable, Advisable, Profitable, and Satisfying.

- ### *Reachable*:

    People belonging to a niche have one thing in common: they hang out or congregate in similar places both online and offline. They are in the same associations, attend the same sort of clubs. They read similar magazines and often the same supplements in the same newspapers. They'll have similar hobbies and visit the same sorts of websites.

    Now, you're in small business so you can't afford full page ads in major magazines or to sponsor major public events – which is your <u>only</u> marketing choice <u>if</u> your clients are diverse. If you narrow your focus, however, to target a single niche then you can direct your advertising and promotions to where this specific group congregates, to what they read, to what websites they go to and so on.

    You can <u>only</u> ever effectively reach a niche with marketing. The most profound words in small business marketing are also very simple:

"You can reach a niche"[4]

- ### *Advisable*:

Gold Clients listen to you as they have been positioned right from the beginning to see you as the expert. They <u>came</u> to you as the authority after reading your White Paper or newsletter, or hearing how you helped others like them (more on these topics later) and you didn't have to go into your hard-sell 'Mr. Hyde' mode.

In this situation you begin the relationship with the upper hand and can then provide the service you know your clients need to achieve their goals. In short, clients will be far more likely to follow your advice or use your product or service in the way they will benefit the most.

- ### *Profitable*:

Gold Clients in a narrow niche have similar needs and require similar services. When you focus on that niche it's easier to sell to them because they know you are the expert, so it reduces your selling effort. It also <u>lowers your costs</u> significantly as you keep providing similar services over and over again. In this way small businesses can start to leverage their time by delegating the work to others because the systems and the processes are set up just to handle this niche. Also you can often negotiate volume discounts and other benefits from your suppliers.

And finally, when you focus on a narrow niche, you are adding more value so you can charge premium pricing!

---

[4] OK, they're my words! But I believe they get to the heart of small business marketing.

- ### *Satisfying*:

Gold Clients (as we have defined them) get good results from your small business because they act promptly on your advice and implement the solutions that you know will work. It is satisfying to watch your clients achieve their goals and dreams.

Identifying your Gold Clients is the first step to creating incredibly powerful and effective small business marketing. To find out more about innovation marketing that works, read on.

Lead Generation to get Gold Clients

If you run a small to medium sized business and you're looking to gain more clients, you will need to dig out qualified sales leads. It *all* begins with sales leads. In the Professions and in other businesses that sell 'business to business', lead generation is the hardest piece of the marketing puzzle.

The three foundation stones of successful small business Marketing are:

1. Deciding <u>which</u> clients you want many more of—Gold Clients
2. Filling a 'Funnel' with potential Gold Clients
3. Staying in touch with your Gold Clients <u>without</u> annoying them

How Do You 'Fill the Funnel'?
Well very simply, there are only three ways to do it:
1. Go where the Gold Clients are
2. Attract their attention
3. Have them sign up for a complementary White Paper or newsletter on a topic they want to know more about

Small Business Marketing Funnel

Effective Marketing in a Nutshell

Marketing breaks down to three core elements, as shown in the Marketing Triangle. Each is explained in depth below.

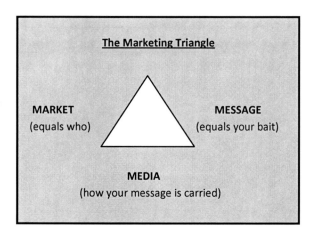

Your Market:

This is your Gold Client, who belongs to a narrow niche as we addressed earlier. When you know who your Gold Client is then you can think of what media to use to reach them, and what messages will make them sit up and notice you. In order to identify your Gold Clients, the things you will need to consider include:

- Who are your best clients right now?
- Are there a lot more of them that you could get as clients (is it a large niche)?
- Which of your services do they value the most?
- How do they think?
- Where do they live and work?
- How do they like to use your services?
- What work do they do?
- What is their education level?
- What cars do they drive?
- How old are they?

© www.leadcreation.com.au

- What are their interests and hobbies?
- What associations are they in?
- What newspapers, magazines, radio stations, websites do they like?

Once you are clear as to which clients you want more of, it's easier to work out how to target your marketing only to them.

Your Message:

Think of the message as 'bait' for your Gold Clients. It is not one-size-fits-all—you need a message that's magnetic only to your Gold Clients. It must also get them to respond immediately by using an offer that appeals to them and makes them want to share their contact information with you—such as by providing a free report or White Paper for them to download online. Effective small business internet marketing achieves this. This process of immediate detail capture gives you the ability to continue marketing to them using the automated system that we will talk about shortly.

Your Media:

Media is <u>anything</u> that gets <u>your</u> message to your Gold Clients. For most professionals and BtoB companies, the main media are seminars, newsletters, industry magazines, newspapers, radio, inserts, flyers, websites, emails, faxes and so on. (One Gold tip about media: faxes really work well. Counter intuitive I know, but they do. And in Australia at least, they are not covered by Privacy laws) Diversification of media is a good strategy to get your message out there.

Using a diversity of media is great for two strong reasons:

1. Different people respond to different media. For example, some people <u>never</u> go to seminars while others are seminar

junkies. Some <u>never</u> read their emails and some live on Outlook or their Blackberry hour-by-hour, day by day.

2. Using only one or two different media makes you very vulnerable to aggressive new competitors, to major shifts in technology and to changes in the laws around privacy. You need to employ a spread of media in order to balance against these risks.

Gold Tip:

The best media of all is the free traffic you get from Google. You can optimize your website to just reach your Gold Clients. And the best news is that virtually none of your competitors are doing it yet if you are in Professional Services or Business to Business marketing.

How the *lead creation* Marketing System Works

What you'll learn in this book is the System we apply for our own clients looking to improve their small business marketing. Step-by-step:

1. We find the 'keywords' people type into Google to find services like yours. We use these keywords throughout your metadata, website content and pages linked to your site so that when people search these terms in Google your website is listed towards the top. This will help you generate leads online.

2. Once people click onto your website they get invited to download a free White Paper that a **lead creation** copywriter

has written on a topic (decided upon in consultation with you, the client) which is appealing to the type of customer you want. It is usually about 20 pages of A4—and yes, we know hardly anyone will read something that long, but that's not the point (more on that later).

3. In order to download the White Paper the person has to provide some of their details such as name, email, job title, company they work for, phone number, post code (it will vary depending on what information we require in order to segment the database, and how much we think they will be happy to provide).

4. Once they fill in their details an email is automatically sent to them which contains the White Paper and a message from you.

5. The White Paper contains valuable information on a topic they are interested in and positions your company as the expert in this field – it shows that you are knowledgeable and that your advice should be highly valued.

6. The White Paper contains valuable information, but its main purpose is as a sales pitch for the product or service that you sell. Every White Paper ideally contains a 'call to action' (we want people to do something specific as a result of reading it) and the White Paper will give instructions on how they can respond to you – e.g. they might call your office or schedule an appointment .

7. Once they've registered their details in order to download the White Paper, they not only get the White Paper itself but also a sequence of 2 or 3 emails delivered over time (say, one a week or one every two weeks).

8. Each of the subsequent emails is sent out with an autoresponder system to the prospect and contains valuable information on topics they are interested in. They all contain

the option to unsubscribe and will not be sent too often or with irrelevant content. We do not send spam as small business internet marketing that annoys people is simply ridiculous. Each email will contain a call to action – e.g. to call your office or an offer for a seminar or a complimentary consult.

9. The purpose of this ongoing process is that people don't buy a $5,000 or $10,000 service from someone they don't know just because they read a brochure or looked at a website – a relationship based on knowledge and trust is needed first. If you send only valuable information in White Papers and emails (without irritating them) then you will be able to develop this relationship. You'll remain in their minds while positioning yourself as the expert in the field – so that once they are ready to commit to using services like yours, they'll think of you first.

To learn more about common marketing misconceptions, visit the video section of the *lead creation* website:

http://www.leadcreation.com.au/lead-generation-videos

Chapter 2: Keywords—The Foundation of Effective Small Business Marketing

Direct Potential Customers to Your Website

'**Keywords**' are the foundation of any small business marketing. They are the words and phrases people search online when they're looking to find products or services like the ones you provide. Unless you know the words your clients use in their conversations and when they search online, how can you reach them? You can't build effective messages into your marketing which taps into their emotions and make them desire your products and services if you don't already speak their language.

Your keywords are the specific phrases that the clients <u>you want to attract</u> use to search online for small businesses like yours. You will need to analyse the many variations of phrases people might type to see which keywords have a significant volume of traffic in your country.

What we do with our Keywords

1. Google AdWords Campaigns

Keywords can be used in a Google AdWords campaign. This is an effective method of quickly attracting well-targeted traffic to your website. *lead creation* utilise a proven technique called the 'long tail' keywords strategy, which means we will advertise on long phrases that not many other firms target, in order to generate leads for your small business. The benefit with these 'long tail' keywords is that when people type them into Google, they're highly targeted in what they are seeking, and are less likely to just be 'browsing'. While there are a lot less of them, they are more likely to be buyers: and there waiting is your website.

2. Embed Them in Your Website Copy to Improve SEO

The trick is to take your keywords and embed them in your website and other areas of your internet marketing without making the copy seem jumbled or unprofessional. Our writers at **lead creation** specialise in 'persuasion copy', which positions your business as the expert in the field and prompts prospective clients to act—see chapter 4 for how you can do it. The embedding of keywords in your website helps Google decide how relevant your site is when someone is searching for those words, and for services like yours.

For example our **lead creation** keywords and the approximate traffic as at October 2009 are:

Keyword	Cost Per Click	Competition	Volume
lead generation	$10.73	100%	4400
small business marketing	$8.53	100%	3600
internet marketing strategies	$5.99	100%	1300
marketing to business	$7.05	73%	1300
b2b marketing	$6.24	100%	1000
online internet marketing	$8.15	100%	880
business marketing strategies	$6.32	100%	590
internet marketing consultants	$6.91	100%	320
cost effective marketing	$5.62	80%	110

The Keyword Comedy Stuffing

Sounds a bit like the Keystone cops from the great era of black and white films!

However, there is a serious point: Many people still think you should stuff your pages with keywords to make your pages rate more highly. Let's look at how they are doing this, with a high traffic term like Small Business Marketing. The text often ends up looking like this, hardly encouraging you to believe they are professional in their marketing, nor engaging you in what they are trying to say.

"Small business marketing solutions—how to effectively use small business marketing in your business. Why small business marketing can work well in your small business. If you would like to learn more about small business marketing, call our small business marketing experts."

At the end of the day, people finding your website is only the first part of the story. Traffic is not the complete answer. Traffic plus engagement is the full story.

This is something hard selling SEO salespeople often conveniently overlook as they hype you on the benefits of lots of traffic. Visitors are just visitors!

So How Do You Find Your Keywords?

The most effective strategy is to use the free Google AdWords Keyword Tool. This was (obviously) developed by Google, and it will approximately estimate the traffic on your words. The key point: it is an estimate, and has the alarming habit of changing, sometimes significantly, the next time you look at the same words. However, what matters is the **relative traffic** between different words and phrases—this tells you where you should be focusing your efforts.

You need to create an account for yourself at AdWords.google.com. You don't have to pay anything unless or until you put a campaign online. You are still able to access the keyword tool without an account.

What about the other search engines? In Australia, Google totally dominates—to the extent that the others are irrelevant. In fact, we have started calling it GO for Google Optimization, and not SEO!

In most other countries, for businesses that market BtoB or that are in Professional Services, Google is by far the dominant engine. However, the techniques you use to optimize for Google are very similar to the other engines.

Here's what the tool looks like:

All you have to do is input the terms that you think are relevant to your company and click the 'Get keyword ideas' button. You need to target your own country if you only market domestically. In Australia, make sure that you target English, Australia, as most people searching in Australia search from Australian IP Addresses or use www.google.com.au.

If you keep churning through keyword ideas you will come up with some logical words that will correctly target your company. You must think laterally to develop words that are correct and accurate for your small business internet marketing. For example, if you were in 'business coaching', then you would not compete on high traffic words like 'corporate consulting'. While you think that this is relevant, you must realize that even marketing businesses like **lead creation** are broadly defined as corporate consultants – in fact, every man and his dog are corporate consultants these days.

A Worked Example of how to Find Keywords

For the purposes of this example – explaining how to locate your keywords, let's pretend your small business is in the Managed Print Service industry and trying to target a specific niche market in Australia. After going into Google AdWords, you would begin by:

Inputting and Outputting Data

To begin searching for ideas, type your initial keyword thoughts into the keyword form (click the radial button 'Descriptive words or phrases' then enter keywords into the form). For your first keywords you should simply think about what the company does. These keywords should be the simplest form of the word possible. The keywords I'm going to try are:

- Manage print service

- Manage print software

- Print solution

- Print cost

- Print company Sydney

- Photocopy service

- Print management

It is best to write one keyword at a time and output them separately as then you can distinguish why Google has recommended these certain keyword ideas.

Below you can see where I have typed in the keyword and formulated the ideas.

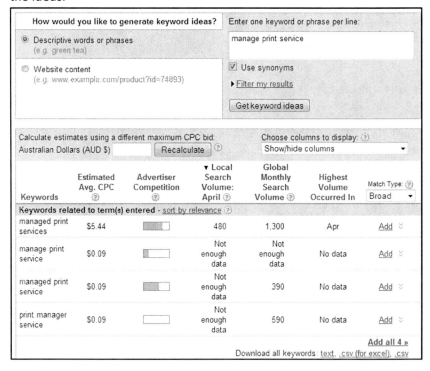

© www.leadcreation.com.au

As you run each of your ideas through the tool, you want to have them sorted by <u>Local Search Volume: Month</u> this is because it is the relevant data for your country (not many small businesses market globally). You should also export all ideas to Excel using the <u>Download all keywords: .csv (for excel)</u> link in the bottom right corner of the output.

The data that you are outputting will be completely raw and untargeted. Now you must read each and every individual line of that data and decide what searches would be relevant for people trying to find you. It is worth it! Finding your keywords allows you to generate leads— without them you cannot market online (and it is even tough offline).

For instance, your output from 'print solution' has come up with about 50 keywords that are not relevant for your search. You should then just remove this data from your spreadsheet. Although some of this data may be useful later for when you're doing an AdWords campaign (a great small business marketing tool), it is not hard to regenerate the search based on the results of your spreadsheet.

Once you have output all data into Excel (and have about 10 Excel windows open) and have deleted irrelevant output, you want to combine all data into the one spreadsheet. The output for your words is shown below.

Search	Keywords	CPC	Comp	Local Vol
manage print service	managed print services	$5.44	73%	480
manage print software	print manager software	$6.97	60%	36
print solution	print solutions	$2.98	80%	1,900
	printing solutions	$8.11	86%	880
	print solution	$3.90	73%	320

printing solution	$5.00	80%	210
print management solutions	$6.28	66%	58
print cost printing cost	$4.14	73%	1,900
printer cost	$4.31	73%	1,300
printing costs	$3.80	86%	1,300
print cost	$3.45	60%	1,000
cost of printing	$4.26	60%	480
print costs	$2.92	60%	260
low cost printing	$5.47	86%	210
cost per print	$3.03	46%	170
costs of printing	$3.22	40%	110
printing cost per page	$2.79	46%	73
photo printing cost	$6.62	53%	58
laser printing cost	$2.92	46%	46
print cost per page	$4.78	33%	46
laser printing costs	$3.96	46%	36
the cost of printing	$3.23	33%	28
print company Sydney printing companies Sydney	$3.22	46%	590
printing company Sydney	$2.17	46%	170
photocopy service photocopying services	$3.39	66%	720
photocopier service	$4.39	80%	390
photocopying service	$4.43	60%	260
photocopy service	$3.43	73%	210

	photocopy services	$3.69	73%	140
	photocopier services	$8.56	66%	46
print management	print management	$7.66	100%	2,900
	print manager	$6.29	80%	1,000
	managed print services	$5.45	73%	480
	printer management	$5.60	80%	390
	printing management	$6.87	73%	260
	print management software	$8.76	80%	170
	printing manager	$3.24	60%	170
	print management Australia	$3.88	26%	110

Remember that this data should always be relevant. Percentages should be displayed as percentages. Data with no value is useless.

To Clarify:

Now's a good time to explain what this data represents and why it's useful for small business marketing. Remember that all data output by the AdWords Keyword Tool is <u>very</u> approximate.

CPC and Competition is only used here as a point of reference. This data refers only to Google AdWords and not to SEO or Google Search. You can however assume that if there is a competition of 100% on a keyword, then that keyword is also likely heavily optimized.

The data that we are interested in is the traffic. Generally a high traffic keyword would be best if the competition was low, but it is extremely rare that you will find such a keyword; so there is a technique to get around this.

The Next Step is to Extend Your Words

Looking at the table shown above, you will see that the keyword 'printing cost' has traffic of 1900. This means that as a *broad search* people have searched for '...printing ...cost...' This may be in the form of 'printing cost' or it may also be in the form of 'printing cost per page', which you can see has traffic of 73. Another search could even be 'what would printing be these days if there was no cost involved'. As long as the search contains these two words, it contributes to this traffic. By optimizing for 'printing cost per page' you are also optimizing for 'printing cost', but you must not add the traffic as the traffic for the 'per page' search is already calculated in the 'printing cost' search.

On the other hand however, you will see that the term 'print solutions' has traffic of 1900 and 'print solution' only has traffic of 320. This is generally rare, but in this case it simply means that the plural has been searched more. By optimizing for one or the other, you will be optimizing for both. You must take this into account when calculating your traffic.

Now using this search we want to find more words that are similar to the ones found already. We will look at the word 'print management' to try to find out what other *broad searches* make up the traffic in that search.

First we use our keyword tool to find suggestions around 'print management'. Now, from our output we can find all terms that contain the keyword 'print management' (using the Ctrl-F function and 'find all' is easiest).

Putting these into a separate sheet we find:

print management	**$7.66**	**100%**	**2,900**
print management software	$8.76	80%	170
print management Australia	$3.88	26%	110
print management companies	$5.72	66%	58

© www.leadcreation.com.au

print management solutions	$5.77	66%	58
print management UK	$3.28	60%	58
print management group	$0.09	46%	36
print management services	$7.37	73%	36
print management solution	$7.01	60%	22
total print management	$3.99	60%	22
online print management	$7.03	46%	16
print management company	$4.24	66%	16
print management system	$8.38	66%	16
print management systems	$9.83	66%	16
		SUM	**634**

You can see that 634 of the searches are accounted for by the words that are suggested. There are probably another 1000 searches on top of this that have too negligible data to show. The purpose of this output was to find another keyword that has much less competition with high traffic. While 'print management software' is probably the best result shown, traffic of 170 is still negligible. Hence our results are inconclusive. Although, what we have found is that the search 'print management' is correctly targeted considering most other searches below it are useful.

KEYWORD EXTENSIONS

Remember everybody searches Google in different ways. Some people search by typing in brand or product names, others search by typing questions, whole sentences, or even by using local slang or jargon. So how we search will be different to another person's, so we need to consider these other variables when targeting keywords. Also consider people who make spelling mistakes when searching—many people do, and there are often consistent patterns with those mistakes.

There are several ways we can extend and increase variables in our keyword list:

- An online thesaurus
- Keyword Content Tool Generator
- Searching Google for suggestions

Thesaurus:

Insert your selected word into thesaurus.com to find other meanings. For this example we will use the keyword ***print management***.
To use the thesaurus correctly we need to simplify any extended or plural words.

e.g.   *"management"*   would become   *"manage"*
       "decided"   would become   *"decide"*

MANAGE
Main Entry: manage **Part of Speech:** *verb* **Definition:** be in charge, control **Synonyms:** administer, advocate, boss, call the shots*, call upon, captain, care for, carry on, command, concert, conduct, counsel, designate, direct, disburse, dominate, engage in, engineer, execute, govern, guide, handle, head, hold down*, influence, instruct, maintain, manipulate, minister, officiate, operate, oversee, pilot, ply, preside, regulate, request, rule, run, run the show, steer, superintend, supervise, take care of, take over, take the helm, train, use, watch, watch over, wield **Antonyms:** bumble, mismanage
Select any relevant words that associate and make sense with our subject matter.

For this example we could use 'maintain'. We then extend the word to become maintenance and include the previous keyword PRINT. Thus *Print Management* becomes *Print Maintenance*

We then insert the word *Print Maintenance* into the Google AdWords word tool generator to view the results. Our results will include the previous data of CPC, Competition, Local search volumes and Global search volume. From this data we can assess if Print Maintenance is a good keyword. Your small business internet marketing would then fairly frequently include this word.

Print Maintenance			
Keywords	Competition	Local Search	Global Search
printer maintenance	93%	1000	14800
printing maintenance	33%	0	720
print maintenance	40%	36	390

You can use this process any number of times to determine the best keywords for your site. Once you have discovered *your* specific master keywords...then the fun starts. You can start embedding them in your website copy and in your metadata and watch your Google search results rank skyrocket. And what does more traffic equal? More potential clients finding your website and discovering your services. This is effective online marketing for small business.

> *There are more than 180 million web pages in Australia alone. If you are not making your website visible, you might as well be printing brochures and handing them out on the street outside your office. OK for the local hardware store, not for a financial advisor whose niche is senior executives.*

What Do You Do With Your Keywords?

Combine what you've learnt here with the information in our Copywriting and SEO chapters to embed these keywords into your on-page and off-page information. You should also consider setting up a Google AdWords account and expanding your list of keywords to attract more targeted traffic. This way, the right client **will** find **you.**

Chapter 3: The Power of SEO—Improve Your Client Inflow Tenfold

Search Engine Optimization (SEO)

There are hundreds of millions of websites currently online with more created every hour. <u>How will potential clients find your site</u> in this vastly expanding sea of information? The cold, hard truth is: if you don't know anything about Search Engine Optimization, new clients *won't* find you. You *won't* be able to generate leads online and your small business internet marketing will be useless. You can learn more about a good SEO strategy in the video section of the *lead creation* website: <u>http://www.leadcreation.com.au/lead-generation-videos/google-optimisation</u>.

"So What *is* SEO Exactly, and why is it so Important for my Small Business?"

Search Engine Optimization (SEO) is the process where you deliberately improve and optimize your website so that when people search for services like yours, they will find you before your competitors. It's the process of making your website appear more relevant in the eyes of Google. What about the other search engines? In Australia, Google totally dominates—to the extent that the others are irrelevant. In fact, we have started calling it GO for Google Optimization, and not SEO. In most other countries, for businesses that market BtoB or who are in Professional Services, Google is by far the dominant engine. However, the techniques for optimizing Google are very similar to the other engines and will work there as well.

If you want prospects to find you, you need to be towards the top of the first results page—which is the first 10 entries on most people's browsers. The simple fact is that the higher up you are on the results page, the more people will click on your link. A ranking on page one will greatly increase the traffic that visits your website. People don't and won't sort through the thousands of entries that come up in their search. Many rarely even go to the second page.

Outrank Your Competitors

Have you ever wondered why a particular website comes up first in your search results? Because they have fantastic marketing ideas? Well, that's a part of it, but it's really to do with a complex algorithm—I think of it as being like a giant formula in a giant Excel spreadsheet—simple, but works for a math genius like me! Google uses this to rank websites in terms of relevance to the particular term you search. Google uses programs that automatically download and analyse all of the content on a website, so that it can determine how relevant a page is to the search terms people type in.

How Does Google do it so fast?

It always amazed me how Google could return search results in a fraction of a second (if you have a high speed connection and a fast PC), and how it could search the entire Web returning relevant results, all ranked in order? **The secret? Google <u>doesn't</u> search the Web.**

They just search their <u>own</u> database, not the Web.

Google sends out robots (Web Bots) that copy all the content on your page and store this in their (rather large!) database. And this content can be old. To find out when they last visited your site, type in your company name, in the results, click on the word 'Cached' on the last line. This shows the page Google currently stores and when they last visited you—your goal with SEO is to make them visit you more often. If your content never changes, they won't have a reason to come back.

Search Engine Optimization Could Be the Boost Your Small Business Needs

Small businesses simply don't have the budgets to compete online with large corporations, **unless they start employing SEO techniques**. If you are a smaller company, potential clients are unlikely to know about your brand, or even your company name, before they search. However, if your website is effectively optimized, it will appear on the first page of Google search results, making it much easier for a potential client to find and click on. Once they are on your site, the copy will inform these potential clients who you are and what you do, while positioning you as the expert in your field. This is what convinces potential clients to use your services – even if they'd previously never heard of you.

What Secrets Would an SEO Guru Reveal to You?

There are two ways of optimizing websites – described as **On Page** and **Off Page** optimization. The appropriate use of keywords is integral to On Page optimization as they are used directly on your web pages. Tips for both these kinds of optimization are revealed on the next few pages for business to business lead generation and B2C marketing as well.

Techniques for Improving *On Page* SEO

- Increase the number of pages on your website. This increases the visibility of the site to search engines

- Use keywords in menu links, if you have a navigation menu. This gives additional SEO significance to the pages to which the links refer—and help you generate leads online

- Use keywords in your URL (your website address)— Google loves it. For example, most law firms use the partners' names in the URL – a huge waste. One of our clients is O'Neill Partners. We bought the URL www.oplegal.com.au for them and having this major keyword in their address has given their new website a huge boost

- Use keywords in the name of an HTML page file, it has a major positive effect on your ranking

- Use keywords and descriptions in your 'anchor text' (the underlined text, the link). Those who know nothing about SEO write '<u>Click Here</u>' as their link, which is a complete waste of this extremely valuable 'real estate'

- Use the Alt tag attribute on images. This provides images with a text description that can be 'seen' by Google, because as mentioned before, the website analysis programs cannot read images or graphics just by themselves

- Make use of your site's Meta tags. These are used to carry information, which can then be read by browsers or other programs. Metadata consists of a title, description and keyword tags

- Use keywords within the internal links on your site. If your navigation menu or header consists of graphic elements to make it more attractive, search engines will not be able to index the text of its links. Your navigation menu/header should be text based so Google can analyse it (though spiky haired young web designers don't want to hear this. You are taking half their fun away. But it's your website, and do you want customers or just to look funky?!)

- Use keywords in headings. Headings are text highlighted with larger and bolded fonts. You only need to highlight each keyword two or three times on a page for it to have a positive effect on your position

- Use keywords in the title tag of each page of your site. The title of your page should be 65 characters maximum including spaces. This shows up on the Google search results page with the description of your website underneath. The description should be 155 characters max. including spaces

- Create a site map of your website to allow search-engine 'spiders' easy access to your entire site.

Techniques for Improving *Off Page* SEO

The main technique for Off Page SEO that small business internet marketing uses is Link Building. The more relevant links your page has, the more visible it is to Google and the more chance you have of getting your website among the first on the search results page.

You can build more links by:

- Joining a forum. This is a great way to get a back link and also obtain targeted traffic that is relevant to your site's theme

- Having your site listed in web directories. There are two main types of web directories available: one is general, the other one is specific about the topic. As far as link building is concerned, both options are useful. In Australia, you can submit your site to directories such as hotfrog.com, DMOZ.com, True Local, Sensis and Yellow Pages among others

- Submitting articles to online article directories. Anybody can submit his or her article to article directories and link their own webpage to them. And remember: <u>increased links to your page = increased visibility to Google</u>

- Creating press releases and blogs. Include links to your site in blogs and press releases

- Exchanging links with other company websites. With this process, you link your site to theirs and they link their site to yours, increasing the visibility of both sites

- Improving your social networking using LinkedIn, Twitter and bookmarking sites. Read the chapter on Social Networking for more on this. It is a goldmine for improving your rankings.

- One other way of improving your website optimization is to use the oldest URL possible. Google prefers URLs that have been around for longer; so if you know what you want your website to be, then register it early and you'll generate leads sooner.

The 6 Steps That Will Improve Your Optimization

Our expert team at *lead creation* use twelve strategies to optimize small business marketing websites like yours. SEO is a complicated and time-consuming process, so here are six of the easier and most powerful strategies that <u>you</u> can implement yourself.

1. Use text appropriately

You need to have a text-based website. Understand that Google can <u>only</u> read text. Google sends out programs that analyse the text on your page, these are called robots or 'bots'. Websites that are overloaded with graphics and flash <u>can't</u> be read by Google—and therefore won't appear in search results.

Text must be used everywhere possible. You can still have a professional website by loading up images (and using the alt tag function) and having a neat and clean presentation. You can still have a nice background and professional colours, but <u>don't</u> overload it with images and flash.

2. Use keywords

Keywords are what your potential clients put into the search box in order to find you. Pretend you are one of your clients and imagine what they type into Google when looking for you.

3. Position keywords in the right places

Keywords should be put throughout your text, but shouldn't interfere with the flow and feel of your page. The place that will provide the biggest impact for your keywords is the Metadata. Metadata includes the 'behind the scenes' titles and descriptions for each page. Implement appropriate keywords on those pages and this will almost instantly boost your page position in search results. Titles must be kept to a maximum of 65 characters including spaces, and descriptions should be kept under 155 characters including spaces—it's all Google will read.

One of the easiest and most effective places to use keywords is in the titles and body text visible on your page. Google's programs read all of this text. Your <H1> (first heading) tags are the most important piece of visible text, followed by <H2> (second heading), <H3> (third heading) and so on, then your link text, **bolded**, *italicized* and underlined text, and then lastly your body text. Your body text should contain about a 2-5% keyword density.

4. Linking and anchor text

The fourth of these six strategies is to use links effectively between sites. If a website relevant to what you do has a link to your site, Google will see this and view your site as more relevant. It is always better to have more links heading into your site than out of it.

While you can't really control other people's sites, you *can* control sites such as your own blog, your YouTube posts, and social networking sites like Twitter, Facebook and LinkedIn and so on. Google visits all of these sites too, so it's a good idea to take advantage of that as well. Linking all your sites will help you generate leads online by improving your SEO.

Don't forget your anchor text. Anchor text is the literal text that you see when you create a link. Use a keyword as your link, not the usual 'click here' or 'download now' links. For example one of our main keywords is Small Business Internet Marketing. So our link might say: "Click on Small Business Internet Marketing for more on this topic." And the URL is hidden 'under' this underlined text—in your Content Management System, you click on the Link button that usually looks like a chain to achieve this.

5. Use Directories

Directories are websites that provide a directory service. Making a submission to them provides links to your website and these are highly valued by Google. The best of all directories is www.dmoz.com, which Google visits almost once a day. Again you should submit keyword 'loaded' titles and descriptions to these directories – 65 characters for the title, 155 characters for the description including spaces.

6. Change your content frequently

If you are frequently making changes or adding or extending pages, then Google notices and will make sure that it drops by to visit you more often.

Have you ever seen the 'cached' link below a Google search result? That shows you what your website looked like the last time Google was there, and that cached result is how Google still sees you now; it's what they have stored in their database.

The more you change your content, the more Google will visit you, which in turn will make your site more relevant.

Beware of over-optimization

If your page doesn't read well, or if you advertise for something that is irrelevant to what you do, people are more likely to leave your page without taking action. This is not good small business marketing and Google can actually track this. Google monitors how long people spend on your page and what they do there. So if people are leaving your page and going elsewhere, Google knows about it and knows that your page isn't relevant. Your site's ranking will decrease.

As an aside, is anybody else getting worried about how much global power Google has? And how much more it is about to get as it successfully challenges Microsoft (in a loose alliance with Apple and its amazing iPhone) and also its challenge to another Gorilla, Amazon?

Small Business SEO—the Laws

Does a small business need to do things differently to the big fellas? Yes, slightly, and here are our small business SEO laws:

1. Google treats every page and every link equally, so ultimately small business SEO is no different. The main difference lies in your strategy. Typically you have hundreds of competitors and so the short keywords in your field are highly competitive— because your budget is limited you need to target the longer tail, lower traffic, lower cost words.

2. If you don't have a niche, don't even think about SEO. Complete waste of time unless you are a giant corporation. How can you optimize for everything? Dumb to even think it's possible.

3. The Google Algorithm doesn't matter to you. It's irrelevant for small business SEO. Neither does the fact that Google are constantly tweaking it to try and achieve its mission: improving the relevancy of what appears when we all search online. There are a couple of fundamental rules that will never change:
    *   Have relevant content for what you do, and that matches what people are searching for
    *   Links to your site from relevant content matters
    *   More content matters

Small business SEO is not complicated, it just begins with your niche. And continues with long tail keywords that have relatively less traffic.

Meta Tags – the Key to Successful SEO

One of the most important factors affecting small business internet marketing and SEO is a webpage's **Meta tags**. These contain information which Google uses to understand what the page is about so that it can show it on the results page of relevant searches. Meta tags can be edited by copywriters in the 'back end' of a website by selecting 'Metadata'.

Meta tag elements include a webpage's:

- **Title** (65 characters long including spaces)
- **Description** (155 char. long including spaces)
- **URL** (65 characters)
- **Keywords** (five or six needed)

How is it done?

1) Be careful how many characters you are using (including spaces) for the title, description and URL. An easy way to find out how many characters a sentence has it to write it in a word processor like Microsoft Word, select the specific text only and click Tools, Word Count and look at Characters (With Spaces). We then leave the Count tool open so we can keep checking

2) Try to use the maximum amount of characters for each Meta tag element or as close to it as you can. Don't just use 40 characters out of 65 – try to use them all as this allows you to put more key words into this very valuable 'Google Real Estate'

3) Recognise that the first word is the most important in SEO terms; the second word is the second most important and so on. Therefore, your first word ideally should be your biggest keyword

4) You can use abbreviations for words which aren't keywords, use exaggeration (explained below) and numerical characters where necessary

Where Do You Go to Edit a Website's Metadata?

To edit the Meta tags of webpage you need to log in to the 'back end' of the site where you can make administrative changes. If you were to edit the Metadata of a site built in the very popular (and free) web site creation software www.Joomla.org, you would:

1) Log in, go to the Content menu and click Article Manager

2) Select the relevant article you want to edit the Metadata for. It will bring up the article and on the right hand side of the page you can open the Metadata info

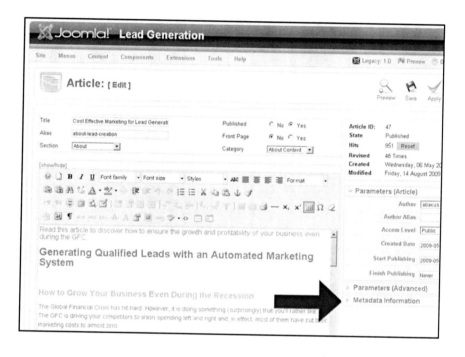

2) Edit the Title, Description and Keywords (using appropriate keywords and the correct number of characters for each field)

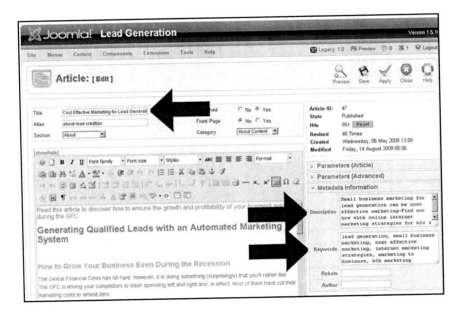

© www.leadcreation.com.au

The Title – The Most Important Part!

The website title is the most important part of the webpage. It is the **number one** factor Google considers when trying to work out how relevant your page is to any search, and it is considered the page's 'headline'. It is 65 characters long including spaces. As with all online text, the first word is more highly valued by the 'Algorithm' than the second word, which is more regarded than the third word, etc. Take this into account when creating a title, and try to use your biggest keyword first or at least early on in the title. It should still make literal sense and also include the company name if possible.

The keywords are the foundation stones when it comes to editing your data. These keywords target the traffic that you want to obtain. Put your keywords up on the wall or somewhere prominent and refer to them constantly for all the different pieces of marketing you do.

Make the Title Descriptive

Try not to choose something like "Welcome To The Website of Some Company." Instead, create a unique title Tag like ours on the *lead creation* site. You will have to write the titles for a number of pages on the site, but avoid using the same title over and over – each page needs its own unique title that is relevant and descriptive to the content of that page. Remember you can also use abbreviations for non-keywords and numbers in titles and this will help you keep to 65 characters including spaces. You might need to use '4' instead of 'for' and '&' instead of 'and'. Using a hyphen or semi-colon can also help keep your title short.

To give you an idea of how this works, here's the title of the copywriting page on the *lead creation* site and a breakdown of how it is made up:

Small Business Marketing & *Lead Generation*-Persuasion Copywriting
(Keyword) + ('&' to save space) + (keyword) + (hyphen to save space) + (description of page content) - 65 characters including spaces

Keyword Box Explained

In a page's Metadata the **Keywords** box is where you list the keywords and keyword phrases that are relevant for the specific company/page. These main keywords should also be in the Title, Meta tag description, and of course in the page content.

You should have **5-6 keywords** in the keyword box for every page, but no more than that for the reasons listed below. Note: A new keyword is defined as beginning after a comma, or when it is written on a new line. So you can have in the keyword box: online internet marketing, SEO. 'Online internet marketing' would be considered one keyword and 'SEO' would be considered another.

Note that a senior Google executive has recently (in October 2009) announced that they won't take into account keywords entered into this field anymore. However, we will still put them there just in case. You never know how it may benefit or if it does at all—Google quite rightly tries to be obtuse about its methods. If it didn't, it would find it much harder to deliver relevant results. As all the marketers would just be 'feeding the formula' to get their stuff at the top.

But it seems logical to me that Google are now probably ignoring this Tag. SEO people were advising their clients to put 50 or more keywords in, and as it was the only Tag that was never visible (Title and Description appear in the very vital search results, and are your prime selling tool to get them to choose you), you could stuff it with junk. And people did, as you can still see it all over the Web. So, it's probably ignored and for very good reasons.

Keywords and Character Count of the URL

Use your keywords in the URL and *please*, make the name consistent with what is on the page and in the title. Tricks to try and get us to think something else is there are very irritating, and unlikely to build trust and a relationship. You can separate words with underscores or dashes as the URL does not need to read well—just to state the main keyword for that page. Avoid having more than 2-3 words in the URL after the /, or no more than 65 characters.

Example of Folder/Directory Naming:
        Bad: "/na/do/"
        Better: "/content/seo-guide/"
        Best: "/seo/free-seo-guide/"

Example of File Naming:
        Bad: "prod.jsp?v=09&w=87&x=65&y=43&z=21"
        Better: "pageID_0987654321.php"
        Best: "free_seo_guide.php"

Description of the Page
This tag is used to describe a webpage and is often displayed by Google on the search results page—in fact they increasingly seem to use it, rather than selecting random text surrounding the keywords on the page.

The description should be specific to the page it is referring to and contain keywords/phrases that are found in the page title and that are relevant to page content. Note: It must read well. SEO is a second priority to this. Always remember to put the most important keyword first. Minimise irrelevancies and put the essentials near the beginning of the description so that the main parts of your description will still be displayed.

The description should have only 155 characters (including spaces) and again should include all keywords possible yet still make literal sense, albeit it might be a little 'clunky'. For example one of our descriptions is:

    Lead generation and small business marketing strategies using online internet marketing for cost-effective marketing to business and B2B marketing

The keywords that have been used are:

- Lead Generation
- Small Business Marketing
- Business Marketing Strategies
- Online Internet Marketing
- Cost effective Marketing
- Marketing To Business
- B2B marketing

Exaggerating text

This is done through using punctuation marks, such as commas, exclamation marks and ellipses. These help separate content and attract Google users to click on the Google link to the page. Using ellipses at the end is a subliminal suggestion to encourage them to click on the link to our website....

How Does *lead creation* Optimize a Website?

The main tasks *lead creation* undertake to improve the SEO of clients' websites (and that you can do for your own site) are:

1. Creating five keyword rich articles for your website – one for each 'master' keyword, each on a separate webpage (a Landing Page)
2. Directories – we submit both your blog and website to directories
3. We submit five articles to three different article directories such as ezine.com. These point back to the various pages on your website and again, Google values this highly
4. Set up a Blog – the prime purpose of this is to increase targeted traffic by creating links. You are not obligated to become a blogger as your company's blog is used mainly to increase keywords and for SEO
5. Set up one or two social networking sites like LinkedIn, Twitter, or YouTube—again for the links

To recap: Implement these 7 techniques to improve the SEO of your website:

1. Have a text-based website
2. Use the alt-tag function to give images a description Google can analyse
3. Change and add content to your site often
4. Use keywords in your content and in your metadata
5. Use keywords in your title and description (65 and 155 characters)
6. Use keywords in your anchor text – don't have the link say 'click here'
7. Have as many links to other relevant sites as possible on your website

Chapter 4: Persuasion Copywriting—How to Make Potential Clients *Want* to Buy

Influence People & Get Measurable Results— Every Time You Write

Successful persuasion copywriting taps into people's emotions and makes them act. It makes Jane or John Smith put down their morning coffee and continue reading after they've skimmed that first paragraph. It's also what makes them interested enough to *want* to hire you or buy from you, rather than your competitor. The art of persuasion is simply about convincing someone to desire to do something you'd like them to do. Easier said than done, of course!

'Copy' is all the carefully written content produced for online and offline media, such as website pages, emails, faxes, newsletters, flyers, posters, advertisements and so on, that market your small business.

> When it's done correctly, copywriting is the single most powerful tool in the small business armoury to persuade potential clients to commit to using their products and services.

Copywriters are an integral part of the success of your marketing, and your small business. A copywriter's job is to grab the attention of the reader, inform them of a product or service, persuade them of the benefits of using it, and convince them to take action in a way that you would like. In short, what they do is to get the message out there, in a clear and arresting manner, that your company offers a fantastic, amazing, reliable and valuable product or service. They make this message believable and credible. Copywriting increases consumer awareness of your small business which generates new clients.

The Benefits of Strong Copy

Copy does the 'heavy lifting' for your small business in terms of developing initial client relationships. The fact is that people simply don't buy a $5,000 or $10,000 service from someone they don't know just because they read a brochure or looked at a website—a relationship based on knowledge and trust needs to arise before they will commit to using your services.

What You Need to Know:
The Nine Points of Direct Marketing

The foundation of all good marketing is knowing what niche is most profitable for your business – the people in this niche are your Gold Clients. Once you know who they are, then every Marketing Communication you write should contain all of these points to be effective and profitable.

1. **The Offer** – This should appeal directly to your narrow niche of Gold Clients. The whole point of the offer is to capture their contact details so you can start a relationship

2. **A Reason To Respond Now** – otherwise most simply won't.

3. **Clear Instructions** – a single clear path to action. This path should nearly always lead to providing them with information and not a sale (just yet).

4. **An Automatic Follow-Up** – consistently follow-up all leads and referrals.

5. **Tracking And Measurement** – done by mostly automated systems so that you know which of your marketing pieces work and which don't. You can then focus your attention to get the results you want.

---

6. **Strong Copy** – you need sales copy that commands the attention of your future Gold Clients and persuades them to take action now. *lead creation* is rare in that we offer our clients great copy as well as providing all the other pieces you need to market effectively.

7. **Sales Are <u>All</u> That Matter** – Repeat: <u>sales results are all that matter.</u> Branding is a nice <u>by-product</u> but is of little value to a small business with hundreds of direct competitors. You are simply too small for it to have any impact in an incredibly crowded market. You don't even need to think about trying to create a brand that is well known, because it's simply unrealistic. What really matters is the excellent service clients get when your marketing system brings them to your door. Great service is what really sells your small business to future clients, primarily through referrals and the all important testimonials.

8. **Know Your Maths** – Work out the Lifetime Client Value (LCV) of your Gold Clients. Remember that a key part of this value is the referrals to other Gold Clients that they will give you. Note that most people when looking at marketing seem to believe that you must make a profit on the first sale – which can be very self-defeating given the LCV is often extremely high.

9. **Attraction Is Proportional To The Strength Of Your Repulsion** – How easily you attract Gold Customers is proportional to how fast you are in rejecting all those that aren't Gold.

   For example, if you are a Financial Advisor and only want to work with people who have investable funds of over $500,000, the right messages will automatically filter out those with less. More importantly, the wealthy with funds to invest will be more attracted to you as they will see you as more able to solve *their* problems. They will see you as a **specialist** for people just like them, and this is a very powerful attractor.

What copy does is spark a relationship between a potential client and your small business. If your copy is relevant to the reader, well-written and has a subtle sales angle, then you will be able to develop this relationship, and remain in their minds while subtly positioning yourself as the expert in the field. This means that when they are ready to commit, they'll think of you first.

A Good Copywriter Using Direct Marketing Techniques and Style Can:

1. Capture and hold the **attention** of your potential client—this is vital because if a potential client doesn't bother to read anything about you, they certainly won't bother to *buy* anything from you.

2. Gain their **interest** through creating engaging content that tells a story and speaks to the reader as an individual, taking advantage of their fears and desires.

3. Arouse **desire** within the reader for your specific product/service by promoting the benefits of it and by positioning it as the best product for them: *the* solution to the problem they've been experiencing. To do this you need to have done some research into what it is your prospect wants and what they fear. You need to tap into their emotions to really engage their desire. The copy should also subtly position your company as the expert in your field, and offer evidence to bolster your credibility so that potential clients can begin to trust you and feel comfortable with the idea of committing money to you.

4. Empower the potential customer to take **action**. This is the most important part of a copywriter's job! It's not enough to only write a pitch that leaps out from the hundreds and hundreds of pieces of advertising that people see every day; it has to go one step further. <u>It needs to prompt potential clients to act.</u> It needs to make them take time out of their day, think about what you're offering, weigh up the pros and cons, decide it's a good idea for them, and then pick up the phone or get online and *contact you*. This is the hardest step, but following the tried and trusted advice provided in this chapter will make it a lot easier for you to achieve.

This four step copywriting formula is often shortened to **AIDA** – <u>Attention, Interest, Desire and Action</u> – and it should be your foundation whenever you come to write new copy, or to reinvent old copy that doesn't achieve its purpose.

How to Write Only Compelling Copy

Most of us will read a piece of marketing – a billboard, an ad in the paper, or a few pages of a website – and think, "Ok, that's interesting" (or maybe the reverse) and then we will go back to our daily lives and forget about it. We are unreceptive to some pieces of marketing simply because they don't appeal directly to <u>our specific wants and desires</u>.

Notice that we haven't said you should appeal to a prospect's 'needs'? The difference is important—needs are different to wants, and **wants** outsell needs every time.

Needs are about necessity and requirement. Needs can be boring, and we'll address them when we're good and ready. But 'wants' make us excited, they make us salivate, they make us think of something far more intangible than just the product itself. Wants address our emotions, our sense of self and our conception of our own status in the world. Wants are related to what we think others think of us. When you really want something — long for it, crave it, hope against hope for it — that gives you a strong emotional compulsion to go out and get it, no matter what the obstacles may be. Appealing to the wants of your target market rather than their needs will make your copy far more compelling and therefore far more effective.

Focusing Your Copy Only to Your Target Audience

What else can you do to make your copy compelling only to your target audience? Using the AIDA formula as described above is a great start. You should also keep in mind the following three points whenever you come to write marketing messages:

1. **Who you want to respond**

2. **Who you don't want to respond**

3. **Offering an incentive that makes people _want_ to respond (some sort of reward)**

First off, your copy should appeal only to the people who you want to respond. Whatever you sell, you need to target specific people, and not just 'everyone'. Therefore the voice, tone, style, language and register of your copy should reflect that audience. It should use words and jargon they use, it should reference things they know, make jokes that they think are funny.

Copywriting needs to contain an element of storytelling, because that's what interests and engages people. You need to tell the story that appeals to your target audience. It's important to know exactly what kind of customer you want because of a fundamental marketing truth: small businesses can only ever effectively reach a niche market.

Secondly, by focusing your copy to speak directly to the life experiences and emotions of your target market, you will automatically be weeding out the kinds of customers you <u>don't</u> want. When people other than your target market read your copy, it won't resonate with them and it won't stick in their minds. But you can also be more specific in your copy to ensure that you only get your preferred customer ringing up to speak to you. You can do this by saying: "This (product or service) cannot help everyone. But if you're x, *or* you've got y problem, *or* (other specific factors), than we *can* make a positive difference in your life."

You <u>can</u> also say, "If you're x or you think y, than we can't help you." It doesn't hurt to be specific in your copy. The more work it does for you in the beginning in terms of appealing to your target prospects the better. As is weeding out those who aren't likely to buy in the end or are likely to be overly difficult customers, the easier your life will be once you start getting calls to the office.

The last and perhaps most important thing to consider when writing copy is what kind of incentive you can offer that will encourage your target market to respond. You can create a sense of urgency in your copy and state that the following offer "will only be valid for a limited time" (but give a good reason for this, a believable and hopefully true reason). You can link your offer to an upcoming holiday – e.g. Australia Day or Thanksgiving or Christmas – to create a sense of this offer being limited only to a specific timeframe. Including a deadline to respond by definitely encourages people to act now.

You can also include in the offer a kind of free 'gift' which acts as an incentive to get people to respond now. The gift may be information or access to an information resource. You might offer a White Paper on a particular topic, one which is magnetic to your target market. Or it may be a free consultation with you. Or you may offer something simply fun and quirky – like a free mouse pad or coffee cup for the first (20 or however many) customers to respond. Deadlines, bonuses and free gifts (even when a little bit goofy) encourage people to act now and help them get over their initial apathy to respond to your marketing. Think about what your target market wants, and about what free gift will strongly, strongly appeal to them, and you've found a sure fire way to get them to respond to you.

It's about *Them*...but who are They?

To write compelling copy that achieves what you want it to, you need to know your target audience. We've included two lists of questions below that will help you target your copy—be as specific as possible when answering. If you aren't sure of some of the answers, you may need to research your target market in greater depth so you can write marketing messages which are truly convincing to them.

Many of the following questions will help you think about the emotional 'hot buttons' you can push to strongly encourage your potential client to act. By speaking to the customer's emotions, you've gone a long way to convincing them you identify with them and that you know what specific problems they face. When you've done that, it's far more believable when you declare that you *can* solve their problems, and they're far more likely to buy from you.

Have these lists somewhere nearby before, during and after you write copy (after is when you come back to edit and revise—copy can always be improved by leaving some time between drafts). Your copy should address the following factors about your niche audience first and foremost, and also be clear and informative about what it is you're offering and why it's beneficial to your specific customers.

<u>To write compelling copy, consider –</u>

Your audience:

- *Who is your main prospect? (Men? Women? Ages? Career? etc – "Everyone" isn't an answer, and won't help create messages that resonate with your main prospects.)*
- *What keeps them awake at night?*
- *What are they afraid of?*
- *What are they angry about? Who are they angry at?*
- *What are their top three daily frustrations?*
- *What trends are occurring/will occur in their businesses or lives?*
- *What do they secretly, ardently desire most?*
- *Is there a built-in bias to the way they make decisions? (E.g.: engineers = analytical)*
- *Do they have their own "language" or terminology? If so, give examples of words and phrases used.*
- *What magazines/publications do they read?*
- *What websites/forums do they visit?*
- *Who else is selling something similar to them and how?*

Your small business:

- *What are all the <u>features</u> of your service? Don't leave anything out...put what you can down. This may take some time but it is worth it.*
- *What are the major <u>benefits</u> your customer gets from your services? (The difference between a fact/feature and a benefit: a fact/feature is something your service does ...while a benefit does something for your customer.)*
- *What type of guarantee do you offer? (The stronger the better. The aim of your guarantee is to "reverse the risk" of customers deciding to choose you to conduct their business.) The*

guarantee we use for **lead creation** *is prominent on our website:* http://www.leadcreation.com.au/guarantee *– check it out.*

- *What's your offer? What are you going to offer as an incentive to your prospects?*
- *What level of service and support do you offer compared to your competitors?*
- *Why would your prospects NOT buy what you're offering? List as many reasons as you can e.g. Is it price? Is it they don't trust you? List them all.*

Establishing Credibility & Believability in Copy

Copywriting is not only about promoting the benefits of your service or product. It's also about convincing your readers that these benefits are realistic and likely to happen for them. The credibility and believability of your sales copy is what will make it effective or not.

There are a number of things you can do to introduce credibility into your copy. **Credibility aspects are to do with:**

- Your qualifications

- How long you've been in business

- Your track record

- Any awards or distinctions you've received

- Your reputation in the field

- Any large or important contracts you've worked on

- Any well known clients you've worked for

- The quantity of clients you've worked for

- The quality of the work you've completed in the past

- Whether you are seen as an expert

For an older audience, credibility will be the main factor that influences whether or not they trust you. Increasingly, however, believability is becoming more and more important to persuading audiences to trust you, listen to your message and even hire you. In order to make your copy believable, it needs to contain justifications. It needs to explain the 'why' behind everything you're offering.

In order to make your copy believable, you need to:

- Emphasise details. Even small and seemingly insignificant details establish groundwork to make your claims believable

- Tell the story of *why* you're doing what you do

- Establish a reason or motivation for your service or product. Tell the story of how or why it came into being, why you thought it was necessary or would help people. This humanises your offering and makes it more appealing. A background story that emphasises why the product is useful also makes your claims of having a great product more believable

- Whenever you offer a discount, you need to explain why you are discounting, and do it in a believable way. You need to justify any discounting or else you will undermine the believability that you're selling a good product in the first place. Perhaps you need to say, "We've done x, and because of this we can pass the savings on to you". Give details and explain how it suddenly became possible to offer a better price. "We need the money" might be true and even funny, but it doesn't do much for your positioning

- If you can get an expert to comment positively on the product, include this in your copy as it adds to the believability

- Use testimonials from satisfied customers in your copy. This shows potential customers that you have previously delivered on your promises to 'people who are just like them', and therefore you will be able to do so again

- Tell stories (recount, don't make up!) of your customers that illustrate your promises actually being achieved. Give details of measurable results within a specific time frame

- If a single element in your copy is unbelievable to your potential customer, the whole pitch is compromised

How to Test Copy

Once you've got your marketing messages and pitch down pat, it's important to consider how your copy sounds and reads. After all if it isn't engaging or doesn't have a good flow, people will simply stop reading. Here are some simple tips you can use to test whether or not your copy reads well.

7 methods for testing copy:

1. Read it out loud to yourself. If you can't read it smoothly or you get caught up or confused between sections, it needs more work. This can happen if you've copied and pasted sections from a few of your documents together – it will sound choppy and it won't be easy to read

2. Have someone else read it aloud – have a friend, colleague or your partner read it out loud. But beware, some people are naturally theatrical and can make even bad copy sound good. Get them to read it out as close to a monotone as you can. If it bores you or grates in places, you need to edit it again

3. Have a grade 10 or 11 high school student read it aloud. This will reveal whether you've used words that maybe the 'average Joe' doesn't use very frequently or that are industry jargon that outsiders, including customers, don't know. Students often have the added advantage of being straight with you. They're likely to tell it like it is

4. Try it out on peers/associates/the office – they will raise objections or pick up quirks you didn't even consider

5. Try it out on another copywriter – but be careful because sometimes other writers can't fight the urge to rewrite the whole thing for you. Explain your target market and ask them to focus specifically on the structure and flow of your piece, and whether it's engaging and convincing. Ask them what they might change or which bits lagged. This will help you get useful feedback

6. Try it out on customers and potential customers if possible and ask what they thought or didn't believe

7. Search for its weaknesses – check things like the rhythm of your copy. It helps to vary your sentence length to keep it interesting. For example, don't just have all short sentences, or all long sentences, or lots of sentences one after the other broken up by the same number of commas. You'd be surprised how much of a difference altering sentence structures can make. To how engaging. And effective. Your piece is—just kidding, but do play around with it and make it different

Making Your Content Appealing & Attractive

The 'cosmetics,' or how your piece looks, are almost as important as what you say. It's important to consider the fonts, sizes and colours of your headlines, subheads, body copy and any tables, bullet points or numbered lists you may have. For body copy in business to business writing you should generally go with a standard, easy to read font like Arial or Times New Roman. Ask a designer and they will say, "When in doubt, Helvetica." (Helvetica is like Arial, basically.) It's up to you, but fonts that are standard in business are what you essentially want to go for. You can afford to be a little more creative with your heading and subhead fonts, but the key here is not just attractiveness but **readability**.

Throughout your copy you should feel free to **bold** or <u>underline</u> important or emotionally persuasive lines of your copy. The point of this is to create a second readership path through your document, and make it more visually stimulating. If a person only looked at the emphasised bolded or underlined points in your copy, they should still be able to understand exactly what you're selling, why they should get it right now and how to order. Think about this and it will help you work out what points to emphasise.

You should also often break up your copy with subheads, and numbered and bullet pointed lists. This is so that the copy appears more accessible to read. If you only had plain text without paragraphs or bold sections or bullet points or subheads the piece would appear unreadable and no potential customer in their right mind would attempt it – even if it was otherwise strikingly good copy.

Bullet points and numbered lists are good because they deliver information quickly, break up long chunks of text, and are visually appealing because they stand out. You should also think of your subheads as 'teasers' which prompt curiosity and interest from the reader and make them want to read on. Spend some time once you've finished your document checking and rewriting your subheads so they're interesting, engaging and fun to read. The cosmetic elements of your piece will go a long way to increasing readership and ensuring that people keep reading.

A Word to the Wise on Pictures

Really good copy is strong enough to work without any pictures. However, pictures will help break up large amounts of text and help a piece to be more visually appealing and effective. If you're going to use one or a few pictures in your copy, make sure they're the best pictures you can find to suit your content. Beware of the stories pictures can tell in and of themselves regardless of what your copy is saying. You need to be careful that a picture doesn't undermine your message.

If you really want to use a picture, here are some quick tips to using pictures alongside your copy:

- The picture needs to suit the pitch

- Use a picture to tell a story, not just because you like it

- Use specific captions for all of your pictures

- If a picture is unsuitable for whatever reason, just don't use it

- Consider the message the picture has all on its own before you use it

- If you want to encourage trust, have a picture of someone with their family, their kids or with their dog – family values encourage trust

- As to where to place pictures on the page, look at where everyone else in your publication or niche is placing them and do the opposite. This will make you stand out

The Fundamental Elements of Sales Copy:

- The copy must be authentic, and tell your 'story'. Throughout history, people have been and still are attracted to stories. People buy from people, and a story in advertising makes you appear approachable and human—you are, aren't you?

- What others say about you is a hundred times more believable than what you say about yourself. Testimonials are the key to really strong copy that causes people to take action.

- Your copy should be long and detailed, and your advertisements may be seemingly crowded with words. Many people say to me, "Well, who's going to read all that? It looks cluttered, who would bother?" Well the answer is simple—it is designed to only be read by the narrow niche that you have defined as your Gold Clients. The copy must be magnetic to them and weed out all others.

- It must contain multiple ways to respond. For example, your copy could contain the option of responding by:

  1. **Calling an 1800 number to listen to a pre-recorded message**

  2. **Going to a website to download a free gift by filling in an online form**

  3. **A call to your office**

It's important that there are multiple ways to respond, and the one you put first and most prominently is the path you want them to take. Why multiple ways? Well, because different people respond in different ways. Some are quite happy to send letters while others only ever send emails. Some will never go to a website and some of us live on them. Allowing your potential client to choose the way they'll approach you makes you more approachable.

The copy must agree with what your Gold Clients think about your services – *'Their World View'*. Others call it agreeing "with the conversation already going on in the person's mind". The more agreement you can create with your Gold Clients, the more you will be able to get them to follow the path you want them to take.

- The copy must present information about, and the benefits of, using your services – hence the copy is quite dense and long. The strength of your message is equally as important as how well it is written.

- Your copy needs to do the **'heavy lifting'** for you. Before potential clients contact your office, the copy and complementary White Papers, will have already positioned you as the expert in your niche.

- All good Copy contains a guarantee, and a bold one at that. One that transfers the risk from your client onto your shoulders. You know your service is good, but your client doesn't until they experience it. So provide an ironclad guarantee with no pathetic clauses that work to make it meaningless (such as "you must return the product in its original packaging", when the seller knows the packaging always gets binned as soon as they open it!). A bold guarantee tells clients that you have absolute confidence in your services so they should too.

If your product is good and you are marketing to the right sort of people, then you will very rarely be taken advantage of by a client. The additional sales you'll generate from a guarantee will more than compensate for the one or two possible refunds.

Remember that ALL business copy you write needs to contain:

- Content which is **relevant to the audience**
- The **benefits of using your services**. It should be about <u>what you can do for customers</u>, and not the other way around. It's not about what you want to sell, but why the reader wants it
- Subtle but persuasive messages that position your business as the **expert in the field**
- A **'call to action'** which prompts the reader to act now and shows them a number of ways in which they can contact you

---

In this next section, we'll provide templates and explain how to write a:

- **Blog post**
- **Email marketing campaign**
- **Landing page**
- **White paper**

Note: You can find out <u>how to write a **press release**</u> in Chapter 10 on Public Relations.

Before You Write, Consider:

1. Who you're writing for – get information on them
2. Promises and benefits of your offer, and how to display them in order of priority
3. Reasons why the customer **won't** buy – address these objections
4. Ways you'll prove your case – employ a lot of different proofs
5. Your offer – know it back to front and upside down

While You Write, Consider:

- The language of your target market, their jargon, their industry experts
- Proof – go in there thinking nobody will believe a thing you say; therefore you must write in a manner as persuasive and indisputable as you possibly can
- Think of your customer as a sloth – they don't want to do anything for anything. They want things done for them. They want the magic pill
- Your job as a writer is to overcome inertia – offer a HUGE promise. Shake them up, frighten them and do everything you can to get them moving, and then make it <u>as easy as is humanly possible for them to respond to you</u>
- Gather information on what is working for your competitors, or alternatively use pitches from other industries/eras—update the language and use these as shortcuts
- When you look at an old pitch you've created, think about why they didn't buy the first time – perhaps they didn't have the money, they simply didn't get it, they were tired, bored, the ordering process was too complicated etc – address the issues and make it easier

How to Write a Blog Post:

A blog post is a short piece of writing published online to your profile on a blogging site. It can be anywhere from 100 words up to two pages long. A blog is used by a small business mainly for SEO reasons. In each blog post, one or two keywords and their variations should be scattered throughout the content. You need to be careful, however, to make sure keywords sound natural in your sentences. You can't just stick a keyword in every sentence or Google programs will penalise your quality score—and readers will disappear.

A keyword-loaded blog needs to be linked to your company's website or be a part of the site. The main point of having a blog is that it will help improve your site's search engine ranking when people type keywords into Google searching for products and services like the ones you offer.

Each blog post should focus on a specific keyword and have a conversational, friendly tone. Telling a story or anecdote is a good way to focus your blog post and make it interesting. It helps to be somewhat controversial or to take a unique stand on an issue. Use metaphors and analogies to make things more interesting. In terms of finding something to write about, you can take content from any company copy you have, like newsletters or reports, and rewrite it in this less formal medium. This will take the pressure off writing new and interesting content every time you come to post—rewriting is much easier and way quicker.

Blog posts are intended to increase traffic to your website and they should also direct potential customers to where they can find more information—so definitely include links. Typically these would be to your main web site, where they can read more, or ideally, download a White Paper. This can be the 'call to action' in a blog post. You want people to do something as a result of reading your post. This is marketing after all, not *just* a chance for you to vent your spleen (although it can be great for that too…)

Tips for Blog Posts:

- Create an intriguing and relevant headline
- Have a punchy opening line – first impressions matter!
- Use relevant keywords throughout the post
- Be opinionated and tell it like it is
- Keep it short and sweet
- Use bullet points/numbered lists
- Proofread and edit before you post – little errors will annoy readers
- Have a consistent style from post to post
- Link to your other sites – primary website, social networking profiles etc. Use the RSS feed where possible—particularly on LinkedIn
- Link to sites that back up your opinion
- Quality is better than quantity – post when you've got something to say
- Invite questions and comments from your readers
- Interact with other bloggers and respond to comments
- Comment on other blogs you read. People may find what you say interesting and want to read more of your stuff, thus visiting your blog as a result
- Timing plays an important role – consider what time is best for the people you're targeting to read a post and experiment to find out for sure

- Try to post consistently, but also give readers a chance to comment and discuss each post as well – finding a balance between posting too little and too often is important
- Use the tags function of your blog to let people know about your topics

Below is a template that will help you visualise how to put all these compelling blog tips and tricks into action. Feel free to base your own blog posts on it.

Blog Post Template:

Catchy, Intriguing Headline to Knock Socks Off (Always use a headline)

First paragraph: punchy first sentence, first paragraph should follow on from your headline. It should introduce your topic and your opinion. You can also begin to integrate links to other sites or to your own sites as soon as they are relevant. Keep your paragraphs short. Aim for one idea per paragraph.

Second paragraph: create segues between paragraphs so the post flows. Think of a blog post like a story: first this happened, then that happened, and always set the scene, e.g.: "Last Tuesday morning was hot…" It needs an internal logic so it builds to an important point. If you just have loosely related ideas one after the other, it won't make sense to readers, and nobody will care. Why not try taking a unique stand on an issue? Controversy is <u>always</u> more interesting to read.

It's also a good idea to use bullet points and/or numbered lists. **Why?**:

- They give people information quickly
- They are easy to read
- They break up long sections of text
- They stop people from getting bored
- They are visually stimulating

Third paragraph: you can also use **bold**, *italic*, and <u>underline</u> throughout your posts for emphasis. A post should be <u>visually interesting</u> as well as engaging to read. The use of highlighting will draw attention to the most important messages in your post, as well as to *keywords*. Google search Robots consider **bold**, <u>underlined</u> and *italic* text more important than other text when ranking the relevance of your page.

Fourth paragraph: Try to avoid a written style that readers will find...annoying. If you use ellipses (...) too often...it looks unprofessional ...and makes your message harder to read. The same goes for excessive exclamation marks and question marks!?!?!?!?!?!? However, by using these elements sparingly and in the right places, they will make a far bigger impact than if you overuse them. Include a call to action in your blog post – encourage the reader to do something –usually to visit your website, or to download a longer paper or a video on the topic.

Final paragraph: Sum up, invite comments, raise questions for readers to discuss, provide links to your sites, your other posts, other relevant material and so on. You might like to mention what you intend to blog about next time if you're organised. An old creative writing technique that helps create closure in a piece of writing is to have your final idea/sentence in the last paragraph link to an idea/sentence in the first paragraph. Finally, don't go out with a fizzle...create a killer final sentence!

Tags: <u>Make</u>, <u>Sure</u>, <u>You</u>, <u>Use</u>, <u>The</u>, <u>Tag</u>, <u>Function</u>, <u>Use</u>, <u>Relevant</u>, <u>Keywords</u>

To get a better idea of what a blog post might look like, visit our blogs at www.smallbusinessleads.com.au and www.tobymarshall.com.

Example of a Blog Post by Toby Marshall:

The Isolated and the Ridiculous –Stories from the Marketing Trenches

Marketing investments by small business are often totally lopsided—and that makes them ineffective and a complete waste of money. It's a bit like buying a clapped out fibro house for $150,000 right on a busy highway with trucks roaring past your front gate; and then spending $100,000 building a pool and entertainment complex in the front garden!

This is what many companies do with their marketing. For example, they'll spend $5,000 on a website but nothing, zilch on optimizing it so that people can actually find it when they are searching for a business like that.

Or they'll spend $4,000 on Google AdWords, but don't have a way to capture the details of their visitors or any strategy to convert them. 99% of them just send the visitors to their homepage, and the visitors are saying: "Interesting, now what do I do?"

Or they spend $6,000 on a PR campaign without first finding their niche— those they want this PR to be read by; and therefore what sort of newspapers and media that these people actually see. So often, PR campaigns for small business are just aimed at profile raising. How will this get them customers when they have hundreds of competitors, some of whom are doing the same thing? And there are hundreds of stories every day—yours just gets lost and forgotten. Tomorrow's chip wrapper as my granny used to say when the press wrote a bad story about someone she knew!

When renovating a house it is essential that you don't overcapitalise it, and don't spend all your money on just one thing like an entertainment complex on a busy highway. With our cheap fibro house, a small pool out the back garden and a high wall out the front along with some good insulation in the walls and ceiling would be a way better use of your money!

It's the same in small business marketing—smaller investments on a range of relevant aspects like AdWords, SEO, PR, etc. Diverse and smaller investments that all follow a pre-determined strategy will be effective.

With our cheap house, minimising the roar of the trucks is surely the main priority. With marketing the priority is lead generation! Why else do you market in small business?
Visit www.leadcreation.com.au for more strategy ideas.

Tags: Small business marketing, lead generation, Google AdWords, Public Relations, online internet marketing

How to Write an Email Marketing Campaign:

No two words seem to terrify small business people who market BtoB more than the innocuous phrase 'email marketing'. They fear this medium because they've seen so many companies use it to spam people with information about products they have never, ever expressed interest in. And that the spammers never give up—sending the same message over and over again. And then again.

They fear that using this form of marketing will only damage their reputation. But it doesn't have to be this way at all. Did you know that an email marketing campaign can be one of the most effective small business marketing tools in your arsenal? It's all to do with the type of content and messages you send out, making sure people <u>want</u> to receive what you send beforehand, and making it easy for them to opt out if they change their minds. Email marketing <u>does</u> work, and in fact it generates billions of dollars each year.

But about the headline—now you may be thinking, 'Why am I learning how to write an entire <u>campaign</u>? What's wrong with just one email?' The point is that no form of marketing is a one off event. It's an ongoing process. Professional marketers say that you should contact your existing clients with relevant and interesting content, and *subtle* marketing messages 12 to 50 times per year. This is just to stay in their minds. Customers don't buy something the very first time they hear about it. They may need to have some sort of contact with the product—through marketing or being reminded of it in another way—at least seven times before they commit to purchasing. This means that if your marketing is a big bang, once-off event, it's likely to be largely ineffective.

The theory behind an email marketing campaign is to stay in touch by sending potential clients <u>content they will be interested in</u>, not to spam people. Whenever a business emails a client or prospect, they must be careful not to annoy them. For this reason, many small businesses aren't confident that email marketing is a good idea. They think it will alienate potential clients and give them a bad reputation. However, if practiced appropriately, it can have a very positive effect upon your sales lead generation.

Why Are Emails Great for Small Business Lead Generation?

1. Sales are driven by how <u>frequently</u> you make a potential client aware of your products and services, and by how <u>recently</u> you reminded them. Regularly staying in touch with prospects and clients with material they value will help you stay in the minds of people not ready to buy *today* but who will be sometime in the near future.

2. Research shows that 31% of people like to be marketed to by email (although they don't mean spam like 'Viagra', of course).

3. It's important to use a diversity of media in your marketing strategy. This is because different people respond to different media. For example, some people never go to seminars while others are seminar junkies. Some never read their emails and some live on their email hour-by-hour, day-by-day. The more media you use, the greater number of prospects you'll reach.

4. If you only use one or two different types of media, you can become vulnerable to aggressive new competitors or major shifts in technology. You need to employ a spread of media in order to balance against the risk of being attacked by an aggressive competitor.

An email campaign works to generate sales leads because it allows you to:

1. Keep in touch
2. Deliver information a potential client might value
3. Develop an ongoing relationship so that the client begins to trust you
4. Position your small business as the expert in the field so that when potential clients are ready to commit, they come to you first

How to Email Market the Right Way

In order to email market to potential clients, and not just get your emails instantly deleted, you need to gain the prospect's **permission** to email them. In order to gain permission to send and keep that permission, there are a few simple things you can do:

1. If you're sending to pre-existing customers, have the first line of email say something like "You've received this email because you are a customer of (your small business). Click here to unsubscribe"

2. Tell prospects that their information will not be passed on to any third parties and that they can instantly unsubscribe at anytime – include this whenever you invite people to subscribe. When there is any question as to whether their privacy will be compromised, people will not subscribe. Have a line which says: No risk, no obligation, no credit card required

3. Have a prominent link on your website that allows people to sign up to receive a newsletter or information on promotions from you. Have a short, simple form people fill out to get your emails right on your homepage, or on every page. Don't ask for too much information in this form and don't hide it away. Remember – the top left of the page is where people look first. Why not place your opt in box here?

4. You can include a pop up on your site that opens and invites people to join your email list to receive more informative content

5. Include links to sign up to your newsletter or other content on your blog posts

6. If you submit articles to article directories, include links to sign up to your email list

7. Make sure you send content that your potential clients will find <u>valuable</u> and <u>useful</u>

8. Offer an incentive in return for signing up to receive emails – e.g. a free eBook or a few chapters of one, software or a trial version, an online course, newsletters, tips and tricks

9. Offer choices of what people can subscribe to. Some people may want a newsletter, some may want an eBook, and others may want tip and tricks. Offering people more choices improves your email list opt in rate.

10. Address people's needs to <u>communicate</u> or <u>learn</u> – these are the two main reasons why people go online. If your emails facilitate either of these desires, you are likely to have more people opt in to your email list.

11. Make sure you deliver on your part of the bargain or people will unsubscribe. Whatever you promised to send is what you send. Don't send too often or too infrequently—let commonsense dictate your timing

12. Make it as quick and easy as humanly possible for people to opt in, and also unsubscribe

13. Include a line in your emails that encourages people to forward the email to their friends/colleagues if they found it useful—just by prompting you may increase your email circulation

14. Include "Join our email list at (your website address)" on any direct mail or faxes you send, and on your business stationary or business cards

15. Whenever you get business cards from others (such as at networking events), keep those from people who expressed interest in receiving more information about your business in a separate place from the cards from others who didn't. Those who asked for more info are expecting a follow up and you can email them a follow up and attach your latest email marketing newsletter. Give them an easy way to subscribe or unsubscribe in this email

16. Don't toss the cards from people who didn't ask for more info! You can send these people a personal email specifically asking permission to include them in your email list. Remind them of the event you met at and explain the benefits they'll receive by getting your emails. Whether they subscribe or not is up to them, but it can often get quite positive responses by sending a personal email to ask. If they don't subscribe, you wouldn't email them anyway, would you?

17. Follow up contacts you met at networking events ideally within two-four days to offer them more information via email. A week is the absolute limit, or else they'll have forgotten you. It's as simple as that. If you don't reach out, your hard work will have gone to waste and you certainly won't get any new prospects on your email list

18. Write interesting, engaging emails!

How to get your Emails Opened, Not Junked

The day and time you send out your email will affect whether or not they get opened. Consider when your recipients are most likely to have the time and interest to view your email and send then. Obviously no one will read an email right away that you sent at 5.30 pm on a Friday. Most people say Tuesday or Wednesday mornings are a good time and that Friday afternoons and Monday mornings are <u>way</u> more likely to attract the delete button. Go with your intuition first and then test alternatives to see whether they work better.

There are two other important factors to getting your emails opened:

1) The Subject Line – "Is this content personally relevant to me?"

The subject line needs to give the reader a compelling reason to open the email. It should be engaging, arouse curiosity, offer some promise of relevant, important information. The more personal and relevant it is to the person receiving it, the more likely they are to open it. Keep your subject line short – ideally between 25-40 characters – so people can see at a glance whether it's relevant. Capitalise only the first letter of each word and don't capitalise small words like 'to', 'and', 'from', 'is', 'it' and so on. IF YOU HAVE A SUBJECT LINE THAT LOOKS LIKE THIS you will alienate your reader with the internet equivalent of shouting and they won't open it.

Curiosity is one of the main factors that drives people to open an email. One of the easiest ways to excite a recipient's curiosity is to start a sentence, then put an ellipsis and continue the sentence in the email body. E.g. "Here is a Method That Helps (your target audience)..." and you reveal the rest of the sentence as your first line of the email. These teasers can be very effective. An unfinished subject line creates great tension, making the reader want to find out the rest of the sentence and thus, open the message.

However, one small caution. A teaser subject line should be composed very carefully. If it looks too spammy, not only does it hurt your open rate, it can ruin the recipient's faith in you as a reputable business.

With all that said, the best way to write a teaser subject line is to use implication. The Subject line should imply that the answer is in your email and tease the reader to open the message looking to find it. Another effective way of encouraging opening is to include a time clause in your subject line to prompt the reader to act quickly and read now, and not just to leave it and look at it later.

If you include <u>certain</u> words in your subject line, however, junk mail programs will recognise them and send your email directly to the junk mail folder. For example, **emails may be automatically junked if:**

- The subject line contains the word "advertisement"
- The subject line contains "!" <u>AND</u> contains "$"
- The subject line contains "!" <u>AND</u> contains "free"
- The body copy contains the words "money back"
- The body copy contains the words "Guarantee" <u>AND</u> also contains "satisfaction" OR "absolute"
- The body copy contains the words "SPECIAL PROMOTION"

You can learn other common phrases which will get an email junked at:

http://office.microsoft.com/Assistance/9798/newfilters.aspx

2) **The From Line:**

This needs to explain exactly who is sending the email. The name needs to be recognisable. Your company name will typically suffice if you are emailing to existing clients or people who've subscribed to receive emails from you. If you're sending to people who haven't registered to receive information from you, this may make them wary of opening, but if you use just any name or your name and they don't recognise it, you may make them far warier. After all, most people won't bother to open emails if they don't know the sender. Be consistent over time with your 'from line' so that you build up brand recognition.

How to Keep People from Going Straight to that Unsubscribe Link

Once you have a potential client's email address, you can send them a series of marketing emails in order to sell them your services. It is important that this information is relevant to what the potential client is seeking—you don't want to spam them because this will annoy and turn them away from using your company in the future.

However, if you send subtle, engaging and informative content to a potential client through an email marketing campaign (most easily delivered with an autoresponder system – more on this in the Autoresponder chapter) you will keep yourself front of mind. When they are ready to commit to using services like yours, they will think of you first.

There are a number of things you can do to maintain a professional standard in your emails so that they won't annoy those receiving them. One simple thing is to include a link in every email to automatically unsubscribe, and be diligent in taking people off your lists if they choose to do this. If you frequently send people unsolicited junk without telling them how they can unsubscribe, they will quickly get very annoyed and you may lose a potential customer. Worse, they may report you to the Privacy Bureacrats.

Another thing you can do is to include the physical address of your company in all your emails to 'prove' that you are a legitimate business.

Most of your recipients will already know this, but it doesn't hurt to have a small reminder just in case they're not sure where they remember you from.

However, it's easy to avoid alienating potential customers. So long as you create relevant and engaging content for your audience, keep your sales pitches subtle, don't send too often and always include the option to unsubscribe, your marketing can be effective <u>and</u> inoffensive. A carefully created email *will* generate leads.

Rules You Must Follow when Emailing a Cold List

A 'cold list' is a list of people whose details you have, who you intend to market to, but who have not expressly agreed to receive any material from you. For business-to-business marketing there are three simple rules we strongly recommend our clients follow when emailing to a cold list.

The Golden Rules of Emailing a Cold List:

1. Never send more than **two** emails. In these emails you give them the opportunity to register to receive more information from you. If they haven't registered after the two emails, you take them off the email list. **Permanently.**

2. The email must be carefully tailored to a very small, very targeted list.

3. Tell them in the second email that this is the <u>last</u> email they will be receiving from you (of course you still have an automatic unsubscribe button). This message must go near the top of the email.

What Should You Email About?

It is critical that your emails are not just about you selling your services. This becomes repetitive and people will switch off, unsubscribe and delete.Your email copy must agree with what your Gold Clients think about your services – *'Their World View'*. Others call it agreeing "with the conversation already going on in the person's mind". The more agreement you can create with your Gold Clients, the more able you are to get them to follow the path you want them to take. Email them with information they're likely to perceive as useful and valuable. So how do you write it?

Basic Email Structure:

It's up to you how you want to contact your prospects and clients. Often it depends on what they signed up for as we mentioned earlier, but in terms of how you convey that info, the possibilities are many.

You can send them updates on your business, or information about new products or services. You can tell them the benefits of existing products or services; you can announce promotions or offer free gifts. You can dream up almost any reason to stay in contact with potential and existing clients. You can have a sales orientated piece or you can use a friendly, personal, conversational tone. You can include jokes, stories or anecdotes. You might like to use a letter layout. You can have plain text or HTML emails (which have nice formatting). The sky's the limit. The way your piece looks is important—almost as important as the words you write. A sales copywriter should have the final say on what a piece looks like because they know what sections to emphasise in order to push emotional buttons.

The most important thing is to keep it fairly short, relevant and interesting to your audience, and not to push too hard with your sales angle. Make sure you include a call to action (you want them to *do* something as a result of reading your email) and offer multiple ways to respond to the email – e.g. visit a specific page on your website for more information, give your office a call if they have questions or to arrange an appointment, and so on.

Tips to Make Your Emails Visually Appealing

The way a piece looks is almost as important as the copy because it increases readership. Cosmetics make your piece visually enjoyable to read. These tips will visually improve your emails and guarantee more readers.

- The copywriter needs to make the cosmetic decisions or check them once someone else has done them
- Use standard business fonts for body copy (e.g. Arial, Times New Roman and so on)
- You don't want anything that looks like an ad if you're doing an email
- Change fonts/sizes for emphasis, put paragraphs in boxes and so on
- Image orientated companies will be more concerned with how polished and professional a piece looks, but often something a bit messy can be more effective as it appears more real
- The more interesting, unusual and fun a piece is, the more accessible it is to readers
- Don't fight the familiar, the colloquial – go with terms people understand
- If a person only looked at the emphasised (bolded, underlined, highlighted, italicised) points in your letter, they should still be able to understand exactly what you're selling, why they should get it and how to order – your

emphasised points create a second readership path through your piece

- Emphasise key benefits, specifics, numbers, great promises, emotional reaction sections – keep giving them reasons to stay interested
- Other things to get something read include using cartoons, jokes, pictures, trivia – these things are attention grabbers to generate interest and also make the copy seem less intimidating
- The form of your email follows the function you want it to achieve
- Don't always let technology dictate your marketing – go with what's most effective
- Typos are ugly, so make sure you proofread!
- If you use a picture, make sure it conveys the right message
- Whenever possible, set your autoresponder to include the name of the person in the greeting of the email. It's a turn off to see, 'Dear Valued Customer', but when you see your own name the email looks more personal and you're more likely to read

Emails of both a Personal and Marketing Nature

You emails should always be targeted to your niche market. You can email your database to let them know updates about your company as well as sending them newsletters or other info. Here's an example of an email *lead creation*'s founder Toby Marshall sent out to tell people he'd shifted from being a recruiter and a marketer to just a marketer. It was sent to a large number of business professionals he counted as friends and so has a personal, fun and conversational tone. It got a lot of replies back inquiring for more information and wanting to 'catch up'. So here's the lesson: keep people updated, be interesting and engaging, and watch the sales leads come to you.

Toby's email to friends updating them on the new business:

Hi guys,

Toby's Rant & First Wednesday are back with a vengeance but a difference! The Rant is now 'Toby's Idea': one idea in each edition – short, punchy and challenging. Plus I have a new book – it will be published on Amazon in November, but more on that later.

I want to tell you a story that changed my life. A story about changing the lives of many young people. And transforming companies in the process ...

They say you can't teach old dogs new tricks, but this one learnt a beauty when the GFC hit ... We were in the boardroom, bit of a panic as our clients were in the hardest hit industry, financial services.

Tough times, marketing budgets slashed. What would make businesses choose us?

Everything changed with one question: "We've had lots of work experience students join us from the USA & Europe, could we find some free interns from Oz?" Long pause ... and then young Sean said, "Why not?"

"We've hired 100s of part time university students for our clients; we could use the same rigorous hiring process on unpaid interns."

So we now have 19 marketing & internet interns, 6 of whom became paid staff. The energy of these talented part timers is an eye opener for old guys like me.

We've spent 12 months creating training processes & systems to make them productive. And it's GREAT for their careers--gaining REAL experience, finding great jobs.

Importantly, each intern specialises in a narrow field—e.g, one only does Twitter. Thought it was just for Twits, & then discovered it was a great tool for raising our client's business profile!

Businesses are sick of marketing consultants who only tell you what to do. With our interns, we implement it, make it happen affordable.

Finding clients for small businesses is my passion—delivering qualified sales leads using the power of the internet & harnessing what could be your goldmine, social networking.

So there it is—my new marketing business called *lead creation*.

But what about the new book? It's called *Lead Generation for Small Professional Businesses* and is being published on Amazon.com. Jointly written by me and our young team, it's a practical guide for small business to improve their marketing.

First Wednesday seminars are starting again shortly, and the theme is on *Marketing and the Internet* – Just for Small Businesses. The first ever event will be announced shortly. Hope you've been well,

Cheers,

Toby

How to Write a Landing Page:

A landing page, also known as a capture page, registration page or sales page, is designed to get people to enter their details into a form you provide in order to receive something from you. A landing page is different to the homepage on your website, even though you may also have a form there for people to subscribe to your newsletter/other info.

This is because a landing page is often 'keyword specific' (i.e. it is optimized around one master keyword and contains this keyword several times) so that when people type that word into Google:

1. Your landing page shows up on the results page
2. They click and 'land' on your page
3. The page provides valuable and relevant information
4. The page also prominently offers the opportunity to get more information, or will offer a free gift or incentive such as chapters of an eBook or a White Paper or a newsletter as an incentive
5. In order to receive more info or a gift, the reader will have to enter their details and subscribe
6. Once the potential customer has 'opted in' to receive email from you, you can market to them

The purpose of a landing page is to get a potential client's details and their permission to send them more information. You can have as many landing pages as you want—each could be designed around a different master keyword, or each could offer a different incentive to subscribe, or different ones could be targeted to different groups and use their specific lingo.

On the next page is a basic template which will help you write a landing page. It includes 'heading styles' which make it easier for your web guy to upload your copy and turn it into a website page. We've used the example of a landing page targeted around the keyword 'SEO' - Search Engine Optimization.

Sample landing page 1:

<HEADING 4> (prehead) Found this an informative resource? Download the free comprehensive White Paper to get more information on cost effective small business marketing.

<HEADING 1> (headline) Get More Potential Clients to Your Website with Search Engine Optimization (SEO)

<HEADING 2> (subhead) A Quick Guide to SEO - Increase Your Web Traffic Today

<BODY TEXT> Body text containing relevant information about SEO. This may go for two or three short paragraphs

<CALL TO ACTION TABLE>

USE NORMAL BODY TEXT

UNDERLINE THE ANCHOR TEXT

WEB PERSON WILL INSTALL THE LINK

<Maximum about 4 lines please>

Final paragraph encouraging people to download or subscribe or call your office – whatever it is you want your landing page to encourage prospects to do.

<HEADING 3> Get More Small Business Marketing Information
<BODY TEXT> Fill in this form to receive your free White Paper

(Your details will not be passed on to any third party)

Form to fill out to download goes here

Here's what the above template might look like one it's put up on your site. Simple and effective.

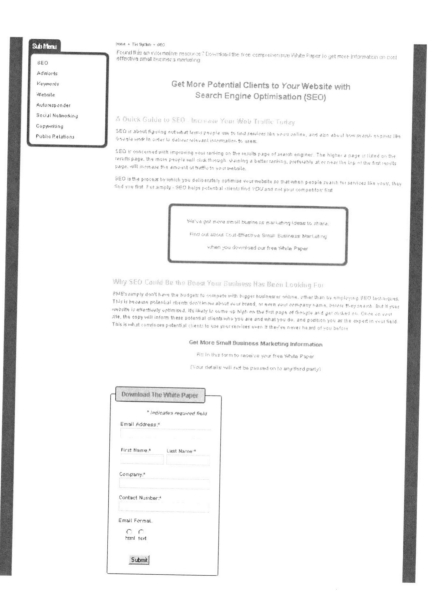

Here's another template you might like to use:

Sample landing page 2:

Prehead

Headline

Subhead

Intro paragraph

Subhead to Make People Read On

Body paragraph

Heading to entice people to skip straight to download

CLICK HERE

Download our FREE White Paper

Subhead

Body paragraph
- **Bullets**
- **Bullets**
- **Bullets**

Heading to entice people to download now

SKIP AHEAD

Skip ahead to receive your free, detailed White Paper

Subhead

Body

Subhead

Final paragraph

Fill in this form to receive your free White Paper today

Your personal details will not be passed on to any third party

First Name*

Last Name*

Email*

Company*

Job title*

SUBMIT

How to Write a White Paper:

A White Paper is a long document which is used to educate readers and help them make decisions. Think of it as a 'big fat report' which addresses a particular issue or problematic topic and provides potential solutions and answers. White Papers are commonplace documents in politics and business, and are a valuable information resource.

If you're like most people in small business, you are now thinking 'Why Bother! Who is going to read a 20 or 30 page report! Waste of time." Well, the simple answer to that is, "hardly anyone, but that is not the point." It doesn't matter if they read it, but two things do matter:

1. That they are impressed with the fact that your small business wrote it

2. That they might read it one day, so they put it aside 'just in case'

Both results are positive for you and your small business. You have entered the conversation in their mind.

A White Paper is used in business in a '2 step' marketing or Education marketing process. It offers potential clients a valuable information resource **before** asking anything else of them. They get the White Paper <u>before</u> being encouraged to call your office and make an appointment, or to buy your product. This information resource shows the prospect that you know what you're talking about and are an expert in your field. Also it appears less pushy and salesey than a single step marketing device like an advertisement where everybody seeing it knows your intent is to make them buy.

A White Paper is a valuable marketing tool because it also begins to develop a relationship of trust between you and the potential client. Developing a relationship is a fundamental part of the process because people *do not* buy professional or BtoB services from a sales brochure or from a typical website that just describes your services. If the prospect doesn't know any more that what they read in a short brochure about you, they certainly won't feel comfortable committing potentially thousands of dollars to using your company.

By providing a valuable White Paper along with other valuable information resources that provide expert advice, you build credibility and trust in the eyes of your potential clients. It also creates a small obligation for the gift you have given them – people generally try to reciprocate for gifts and so are more likely to be open to having a meeting with you or to taking another step down the path to buying.

You can download the *lead creation* White Paper to get an idea at: http://www.leadcreation.com.au/about/whitepaper.

Below is a template for what your basic White Paper might look like:

Page one is a title page. Here's a sample one of ours:

Or you can keep it simple like this.

Headline to Attract the Attention of Your Target Market

Give a Compelling Reason to Read

A line that taps into the emotions of the reader and compels them to seek more information

© www.leadcreation.com.au

Page 2 should look something like this:

Contents

(And so on as you accumulate more subheads)

To format a table of contents in Microsoft Word, you need to apply Heading 1 to your main heading and then format the font style, size, bold etc, and then Heading 2 to your subheadings, and then format the font style, size bold etc, and Heading 3 to any other section headings. It's easiest to start doing this as you write your document rather than going through once it's done and applying the headings.

Once the heading styles have been applied, click on the empty table of contents page you've created and click the Insert menu, click Reference, and click on Indexes and Tables. This will open a box – click on the Table of Contents tab. You want all the boxes ticked, and the tab leader as dots, format from template, and show levels 3. If you have more than 3 heading levels you can change that so the others show up too. Click OK and this will bring up your table of contents. If you add more headings in your document later you can right click anywhere on your table of contents and click Update Field and Update Entire Table.

Prehead goes here in Arial 13 and usually finishes with 'read on...'

Headline Goes Here in Georgia Bold Size 20 (Right Click, Font, Add Shadow)

Subhead Goes Here – Important Words Capitalised in the Headline and Subheads

The first paragraph is your introduction to the topic. It should call attention specifically to the people you want to be reading this document. Different types of readers look at the same problems from different perspectives so make sure your slant is sympathetic to the opinions of your specific target audience. This first paragraph should be informative, yet engaging and **it should start to hit some emotional buttons**. This first paragraph should set up what you're going to be talking about in the article and why your specific target audience really, really needs to read it. Body paragraphs should be Arial size 12 font, and justified. Justify is the fourth button in the text alignment menu. As shown below:

> **Headline – bold**
>
> White Papers contain useful information for the reader but they are also designed to try to *sell* them something. We usually include a box like this in the first half of the first page in calibri size 11 which basically says that the information contained in this Paper is very useful, and there is far more we can give you _or_ we have a great product you would like. It ends with: You can contact us on p: (02) phone no., f: (02) fax no., or e: john@smallbusinessmarketing.com.au

Alternatively, and much better generally, the box should contain a client testimonial. Note that this box is in the top half of the page. In marketing speak it is 'above the fold'. That is, even on a small screen people will see it immediately when the page opens.

Subhead Goes Here & Gives the Reader a Reason to Read On

The first character in the first paragraph was a drop cap. You create a drop cap by selecting the first character of the first word and clicking the format menu, then clicking drop cap, then selecting 'dropped' and specifying three lines, and Times New Roman font. Feel free to bold or underline important or emotionally persuasive lines of your copy. The text spacing is 1.25. Click spacing, more, in Line Spacing select Multiple and set it as 1.25.

Since your White Paper is likely to be quite long (anywhere from 20-30 pages or much more), you should include relevant diagrams or pictures, tables, graphs, bullet points, numbered lists and so on to break up text and make the pages more visually interesting and readable. Use interesting and catchy subheads to guide readers through the text.

If you have quite a few bullet points, number some instead as it makes it easier to read. To make bullet points or numbered lists more engaging if you've already used a few before, you may want to put a box around the bullet points, put them in a different font/size, or put a coloured screen behind them.

As a writer it helps to be considerate of the needs of your audience, and to try to engage and entertain them whilst you inform them. Cosmetics play an important role in this so use whatever different techniques you can.

What *lead creation* can do for You

So if you've read through this chapter and thought, "Man, that's a good idea, but where am I going to find the time?" Why not let *lead creation* do it for you?

At *lead creation*, we provide our clients with experienced copywriters to rewrite your existing content, and create content which is both engaging and persuasive to your potential clients. We are probably the only boutique marketing company in Australia that offers great copy as part of our marketing services to small service businesses.

We usually create approximately twenty pieces of strong copy for clients to use in their marketing, including:

- **Website pages which position your small business as the expert in the field**
- **Landing pages which capture potential client information so you can market to them**
- **White Papers**
- **Email campaigns**
- **Fax campaigns**
- **Blog posts**
- **Newsletters**
- **Advertisements and so on**

Our service also focuses on dramatically improving your search engine rankings in order to direct more free traffic to your company's website. We find the most relevant keywords for your small business and embed them in your website's copy without making it sound jumbled or unprofessional. The embedding of keywords improves a website's ranking in Google search results when people type in those particular words.

Chapter 5: Positioning Statements for Your Small Business— How to Present Yourself as the Expert

We are not what we do – but we need to be able to answer the question, "What do you do?" in a way that makes us better known and creates more business.

> "Work harder on being memorable! A great positioning statement and self introduction needs to be well-designed and delivered with impact."
>
> — Matt Church, CEO of Sydney's Thought Leaders
>
> — **www.thoughtleaders.com.au**

What is a Positioning Statement?

Matt Church has created a nine-step positioning process which achieves two things; first, it enables you to consistently answer the question, "What do you do?" with an appropriate level of detail. And second, it enables you to create a flexible statement that can be creatively applied in different situations.

An effective positioning statement is a flexible statement you can tell people when asked the question, "So what do you do?" at a networking event, a convention or seminar, at a function, in a supermarket queue or anywhere else. This line will convey:

1. **Who you specialise in working with; what industry, and what specific types of people**
2. **How you help these people to do something specific – satisfy a particular need, achieve a measurable goal, avoid a certain consequence**

Your positioning statement will be <u>specific</u>, descriptive and will convey your expertise in your field. It will spark conversations with others, allowing them to get a detailed idea of who you are and what you do, and will encourage others to remember and recommend you with confidence.

The Three Situations to use Your Positioning Statement In

Your statement is a verbal summary of what you do which engages and interests the person you're speaking to. Of course, how you speak will be different in different social situations. For example, you don't speak in the same way to your kids as you would to your boss; or to your child's teacher as you would to your buddy from work. Our language, register, formality, energy and tone all change depending on where we are and how comfortable we feel in any particular situation.

You can create different positioning statements to use in different situations. The aim of having a great positioning statement to use in any situation is to always be able to project confidence and 'sell' your small business wherever and whenever you might meet an interested party— and this is not always at a networking event or in the meeting room of your office. Great positioning statements, tailored to your current context, help you always be prepared to convince your next potential customer that you provide a fantastic service. Don't let an underprepared sales pitch stop you from seizing rich but unexpected opportunities to promote your small business wherever you find them.

Below is a table that will help you decide upon what kind of position statement you'll need for different kinds of contexts or events. You can change your focus, energy and pitch depending upon where you are. An all out hard sell is unlikely to impress someone you met at a party. But it might work on a potential client who just needs a touch more convincing in order to buy.

The three options for the focus of your position statement are: YOU, IT, or THEM.

- YOU is obviously all about <u>you</u>, who you are, what you have done, and what are you into.
- IT is all about the <u>activity</u>, examples of how it has worked for someone, what it is like and maybe a few good stories about what it is you do.
- THEM is all about the <u>outcomes</u> that your customers and clients achieve. You may ask questions, identify the key challenges they face or even get into solutions.

Which to use when:

SITUATION	FOCUS	
Social Event	Personal	YOU
Business/Professional Networking Event	What Activity You Do	IT
Talking to a Business Prospect	Outcomes & Benefits	THEM

How Much Energy?

Overlaying the three situations are energy levels – whether the situation is best suited for high, medium or low energy.

We have provided in this article a table which helps you to create your own positioning statements. We have three versions of this table:

1. The first describes how it works.
2. The second is filled out for our business, **lead creation** to give you a working example.
3. The third has been left blank for you to fill in with your own positioning statements.

Table 1) How Matt's Positioning Statement Table Works (with examples from different companies):

YOU: Talking about **You**	IT: Talking about **What Activity You DO**	THEM: Talking about **Benefits & Outcomes**
High Energy	**High Energy**	**High Energy**
Here you get to talk about your passion. Perhaps rant a little about what it is you believe. E.g.; Toby Marshall: *"I want to make a difference to the lives of young people and give them a great start to their careers."*	Here, you try to set yourself apart from others in your field. State your unique selling proposition and make a distinction between yourself and others. Whatever the masses are doing, try to position some part of what you do as contrary/opposed to this.	This is where you express the client's reason for being in a way that shows you are aligned. You express how what you do is a perfect fit for their purpose.
Medium Energy	**Medium Energy**	**Medium Energy**
This is a black-and-white answer to the question of what you do – answer with a professional category. E.g.: *"I am a Financial Planning Advisor."*	<u>Analogy</u>: this channel is useful if you sell an intangible service or a new category of product or service. You draw a comparison between an already established concept and what you do. E.g.: *"We are like a sports management company for information experts"* – Matt Church	Think about your client's problems. A problem is best described as the day-to-day internal dialogue your target has around what they do. When you start speaking about what's on their mind they truly engage with your products and services.

Low Energy	Low Energy	Low Energy
This is a <u>short</u> verbal resume outlining where you have been and what you have done.	Choose an appropriate client case study, an example of someone you have been working with lately and tell the story.	This is similar to a case study or example, but here you actually state the benefits you create for others. It's often easy to ask a question that explains why you have created a certain solution.
E.g.: Matt Church: *"I grew up in Newcastle, moved to Sydney to study, graduated in the late eighties and went to work in a prison. I then worked for the Australian Council for Health and Lend Lease, wrote a few books and ended up here on the corporate speaking circuit."*		E.g.: *"Do you find that you are spending too much time stuck in the day-to-day running of you business? We have created a personal effectiveness system that allows most people to get more done in less time. Our average client finds an extra three days' productivity per month when using our system."*

© www.leadcreation.com.au

Table 2) The Positioning Statement Table filled out by Toby Marshall as the Director of *lead creation*:

YOU: Talking about You	IT: Talking about **What Activity You DO**	THEM: Talking about **Benefits & Outcomes**
High Energy "I implement marketing systems for small business. The problem is that every professional business focuses on *sales*, but it's **marketing** that's more important. Sales involves a lot of a business owner's time, while marketing positions you as the expert in your field—*marketing* is what gets you qualified leads. **Our system can transform a small business.**"	**High Energy** "I'm a marketer with a big difference. Thousands of marketers can tell a business what to do, and hundreds tell you how to do it, but *lead creation* is the only one that does it for you. We literally implement everything a small business needs to market successfully. No one else comes close to what we offer for such a low price."	**High Energy** "We create an automated marketing system for small business—I'm also in small business and know how critical it is to generate leads—particularly when you have a great service but not enough people know about it. We don't just tell our clients what to do—we implement a complete system that grows your business—and is 100% guaranteed."
Medium Energy "We are marketing specialists who implement automated and integrated marketing systems for small to medium sized	**Medium Energy** "We implement marketing systems for small businesses and it's a bit like a game of chess. You can't rely on just one piece to win a chess game. You need a number of pieces working together.	**Medium Energy** "We create a marketing system for small professional businesses— the biggest problem they face is people won't buy a $10,000 service from a brochure or webpage.

© www.leadcreation.com.au

Services businesses."	Chess and marketing are complex games that not everyone has a talent for or the patience to learn. They require specialised knowledge which is where we come in. We deliver marketing systems, <u>implemented systems</u>, that deliver quality leads. And that's checkmate!"	People are <u>always</u> going to be at different stages of being ready to buy your service. You need to keep in touch with those who are 'just enquiring', so when they <u>are</u> ready to commit, your services are top of mind. Our system does that, <u>guaranteed</u>."
Low Energy "I implement automated marketing systems for small business and its been a bit of a journey: In 2004 I started training under some of the world's best Direct Marketers. This was also the year that I started to use <u>interns</u> in my business model—a creative, low cost workforce. These two developments lead me to launch **lead creation** in 2008—we <u>implement</u> automated marketing systems at a low cost."	**Low Energy** "We implement automated marketing systems for small businesses. For example, an insolvency lawyer wanted small regional accountants and lawyers in NSW and the ACT to think of them when one of their clients was in financial difficulties. To be top of mind, to come to our insolvency client first, without having to spend any time selling. We are implementing an automated system, and one that had to cost less than $12,000."	**Low Energy** "We implement an automated marketing system for small service businesses – one that delivers qualified leads. We've created a system which saves you selling time, and allows you to concentrate on your high value work—building relationships of trust with your clients. Our system is <u>guaranteed</u> to get our client's leads."

Remember: These have to be spoken, not read from a page. So practice speaking, and then edit them to make them more colloquial. Underline the words you want to emphasise.

© www.leadcreation.com.au

Table 3) Your Positioning Statement Table:

YOU: Talking about You	IT: Talking about **What You DO**	THEM: Talking about **Benefits & Outcomes**
High Energy	**High Energy**	**High Energy**
Medium Energy	Medium Energy	Medium Energy

Low Energy	Low Energy	Low Energy

Chapter 6: Websites—Your Prospects' First Glimpse

This chapter will probably upset a whole industry: Web designers. But that can't be helped given that the work they do does an <u>incredible</u> amount of damage to small business. And the reasons for this and the consequences for the marketing of small business need to be brought into the open. A website is incredibly important for advertising your small business, but <u>not</u> the sort of websites web designers persist in creating.

The Tragedy of Web Designers

Web Designers are being impacted by technology shifts like many other trades and professions. The industry became a **lot** smaller, and many of the current players will soon vanish. Essentially web design grew up as a cottage industry—thousands of small businesses in inner city warehouses and terrace houses. Lots of young people and lots of piercings and spiky hair involved.

The industry grew up around people setting up small businesses, often with just one or two staff and then creating websites for clients using the various software applications available. Most of them built little templates that they then used to create the sites, and would customize them for a fee. And every time a client wanted to make a change or add some new function, it would take them a few (or many) hours, at an exorbitant rate. So the clients would only do it if they had to and most ended up with unchanging, static sites; the sort that the all-important Google hates.

Meanwhile technology was bounding ahead, and huge open source platforms were being created. And thousands of programmers were adding to these platforms, perfecting them and writing applications, modules and templates to make these free platforms more powerful. Building websites for SMEs was suddenly <u>really</u> easy and they could do things that even the websites of multinational corporations couldn't do six or seven years ago.

And back in the funky warehouse, the now not so young designer is looking increasingly like a dinosaur as all the new powerful low cost and free plug-ins don't work in their templates.

The tragedy is <u>not</u> that they are going out of business. The tragedy is the millions of small businesses like my mate Ralph...

The morning that I'm writing this (Oct 19th 2009) he was proudly showing a group we are both members of his new website and we all agreed it looked pretty good. After the meeting I asked him what the backend was and what the site had cost. Now the price was ok as it was quite a big site – just $2000.

The problem was it was created from scratch by a couple of students working out of their inner city terrace house. Unfortunately this site needs to be updated at least every two or three weeks as new information becomes available – I asked how they were going to update it, and his answer was that the students would do it for him! What a nightmare of ongoing time and money waste that he doesn't have the ability to edit and add pages himself. He doesn't have access to his own Content Management System, or CMS.

Without a CMS the process is really cumbersome: He has to book time with them; write and then send the copy and the photos; then liaise with them for when it is up; review and edit it; send it to them; then approve the final copy.

As these web designers are students, which is where the low cost appeal has come from in the first place, he has to wait for them to be willing to even do business when it suits them.

All a website for an SME has to have is:

- A neat and professional look
- The ability to capture contact details in a database that can be sorted, emailed, exported, etc
- The ability to send visitors who register an email or email sequence
- A blog built into the site
- A really simple, "even my 80 year old technophobe uncle can use it" editing system (a CMS), where even he can create new pages

This isn't hard to achieve, and it all this functionality can be done free of charge. One of the best <u>free</u> platforms for building and running a website (easily, we swear) is Joomla! (www.Joomla.org).

As a small business owner or manager, don't make the web designer's tragedy yours! We build all our client's sites in Joomla and they have full functionality. And $2000 would be a **big** website for us.

A Cost-*Effective* Website <u>Without</u> a Designer

Small Business Owners and Managers: **save yourself money**. Don't hire a designer at the *start* of creating a website. Contrary to popular belief, <u>the very *last* stage</u> of website development should be gaining aesthetic advice from a designer. Hire one once you've finished putting together a highly optimized site just to tidy things up a bit. There won't be much work for them at this point, because you'll have created a website from one of the hundreds of free and professional looking templates on a free site like Joomla (we'll teach you how in this chapter), and so by then their services won't cost you an arm and a leg.

As we will see later on, there is a simple analogy to how easy it is to use a template rather than have a designer recreate the wheel. Website designers will create custom sites that don't fit within a template. Instead, choose the template first and have the designer make his sections fit inside.

Website and Blog Registration Guide

If you haven't already got a site, then the first step will be to register your domain. This guide will hopefully make this process much easier for you to do this yourself.

1. Registering Your Domain

You must register your domain name with a registrar. This is a website where you can reserve your web address. We have found that www.CrazyDomains.com.au is one of the best Australian sites to do this. You can however use a different registrar—all registrars offer pretty much the same service just at different prices. Once you pick a registrar, you can type addresses into their search tool to see if those site names are available.

Registering a domain usually costs around $15 per year. We suggest that you use a web address that actually has significance to your business function and your keywords. So if you are a certified financial planner you would want the address: certifiedfinancialplanner.com.au.

If you are an insolvency lawyer you would want the address: insolvencylawyers.com.au. It positively impacts on your ranking in search results.

2. Hosting Your Domain

Now that you have a registered domain you need a host. A host is someone that gives you storage space on the internet, so this is where all the images, multimedia and html, php, css and other scripting functions of your website are stored. If you already have an active website it is obviously hosted somewhere. Hosts often allow you to host several domains with the one hosting plan, so this is a good way to save a little money. If you don't have a live host, you will have to choose one. These don't necessarily have to be in Australia.

We have found HostGator.com to be one of the best value hosts ($6 per month) with the best support. You can also often host with your domain registrar to make things easier. However, many are technically backwards and are not capable of hosting the new generation software like Joomla, so be sure to check this out before you go signing up.

3. Connecting Your Registrar to Your Host

So once you have found your host you will have to find out what the 'Domain Name Servers' (DNS) for the host are. This is just a web address to link to their servers. For HostGator.com the DNS looks something like ns441.hostgator.com. If you login to your hosting plan you will often be able to find these details, otherwise you can contact support. To link your registrar to your host you will need to go back to your domain registrar, login to that account, and redirect your DNS to your host. There should be a menu item for this and this will generally take about 48 hours to synchronize.

4. Uploading Data to Your Site

Often your host will have a control panel or a backend login section where you can make changes to your website. This often looks like leadcreation.com.au/cpanel. You should find the username and password for this and keep them safe. This is where you upload data to your website.

Okay, so a quick recap: Your domain registrar is where you reserve your online real estate (www.mydomainname.com). Your host is where all the data of your website is stored (images and other files). To connect the two with each other, you must let your registrar know the DNS of your host.

What is Content Management? And Who Cares?

Websites today have become a simple commodity that is cheap and easy to create. They should also be simple to maintain. You can do this yourself with a good Content Management System (CMS), like Joomla, which even a technophobe can use to manage their site. A CMS is a type of web-based software that makes updating content to your website much easier. Without one, you'd need to understand how HTML and other scripts work in order to make changes, or hire someone who does. But you really don't need to waste that kind of valuable time or money.

Content management keeps track of every piece of content on your website. It is the set of processes and technologies that make the changing nature of digital information possible. This information is often called digital content, and consists of all the text, image, audio, video and other files that exist in the digital space. A CMS allows you to effectively manage all of your digital content.

For your own website you can use a CMS for creating and managing HTML content. CMS software allows users with little or no knowledge of programming or mark-up languages to make and manage digital content relatively easily. A CMS allows you to make changes on your website by creating new content, organising and managing existing content, editing, and maintaining other essential web functions—and is similar in ease to using a word processor. It also stores your digital content, metadata and anything else necessary for the running of your website. You access it through your internet browser. It allows you to present your content to visitors to your site in a number of customised ways through the selection of different templates.

You may need an experienced coder to set up and add features with some CMS but even if you've never had any experience with building your own website, a CMS will give you the freedom to <u>update and maintain</u> a professional looking website without the use of a web designer. Depending on the skill of the CMS engineer, adding pages and subpages can also be a very simple process. When it is done correctly, you will only need to publish a new page under a certain category, and all aspects of the website navigation will be automatically updated, including the main navigation, footer navigation, and site map.

However, if you feel you don't ever need to update your content, then a CMS might not be right for you. At *lead creation* we strongly advise you to use one though, because a site which is infrequently updated will not be optimized, and therefore will rank poorly in the search results of Google when potential clients are searching for products or services like yours. Make your small business easy to find by optimizing and updating regularly. You can do this cheaply and quickly yourself with a good CMS.

How Content Management Happens, in a Nutshell:

Content management is collaborative process that often takes the following form:

1. **Creator** – digital content is produced by one or more authors
2. **Editor** –content is edited so it is appropriate for the website and the target audience. Ideally it's a separate person—as they will far more easily see things that need editing
3. **Publisher** – releases the content upon the website (easy with Joomla)
4. **Administrator** – responsible for managing access permissions to folders and files, usually accomplished by assigning access rights to user groups or roles. They may also assist and support users in other ways

So Why Our Recommendation – Joomla?

We recommend that you use an online processing Web CMS such as Joomla, for ease and efficiency. In our experience, we have found Joomla allows for simple but dynamic programming, advanced user privileges, and easy posting and editing of content. It also has many attractive, professional templates and is straightforward to use.

Joomla includes features such as page caching to improve performance, RSS feeds, printable versions of pages, news flashes, blogs, polls, website searching, and language internationalisation. There are also over 4,000 extensions for Joomla available via the Extensions Directory to improve the functionality of your site.

Joomla is used in many locations across the globe to power all different kinds of websites. It is used for many small business websites, non-profit

© www.leadcreation.com.au

and organisational websites, school websites, and corporate websites, such as the Harvard University site http://gsas.harvard.edu and the Citibank intranet. The popular quiz site http://www.quizilla.com is also managed with the Joomla system.

Joomla is designed to be easy to install and set up even if you're not an advanced user. It also has a vast community of over 200,000 friendly users and talented developers who you can consult if you're having any issues getting used to the software.

To access this free and simple software, go to www.joomla.org and read the 'Getting Started with Joomla' guide to find out the basics. You can also try out an online demo before you download the latest version to see if it's right for you.

There is one over-arching reason why Joomla is better than the rest; it's open-source. There is quite a lot of confusion around what open-source actually is. Open-source (although free) is not a 'shareware' or 'trial' piece of software. It is actually created and governed by a corporation and allows users to create programs and add functionality.

The way this works is the base program (the platform) is completely seamless and created by a programming company. Users then add small functionality packages that improve existing functions and add new ones. There is such a large discussion around this, and so many people working together on improving functionality that each program is precisely rated on how well it works. Most importantly, if you can do anything online, you can definitely do it on Joomla.

What Can You Do with a Web CMS like Joomla?

- **Edit Content Easily**
  Most WCMS software includes editing functions which allow you to make and edit content without technical knowledge. Once content is separated from the visual presentation of a site, it typically becomes much faster and simpler to edit

- **Apply an Automated Template**
  You can put your existing and new content into a template which will change the appearance and presentation of it on your site

Manage Your Documents
Some CMS allow you to manage a document's life cycle. Keep track of the initial creation time, revisions, publication date, have an archive of old copies, and a record of deleted documents

- **Manage Your Workflow**
  This will help you make sure that content doesn't go live before it's supposed to. A content creator may submit content, but through your CMS you can make sure that it doesn't get published until the copy editor fixes it and an editor approves it

- **Manage Delegation**

  You can allow various user groups to have limited privileges over content on your website with a CMS, therefore spreading the responsibility for content management. If you're worried about losing control over content, don't worry, any good CMS can require updates to be approved by an editor before the change is made on your site.

- **Manage Content Yourself**

  An important element of a CMS is the ability to manage versions of content as it is created, worked on, and modified over time. You may need to change content or go back to an older version of it if for whatever reason some undesirable changes are made to it. A CMS will allow you to do this without calling in a designer to do it for you

- **Limit Disasters**

  A CMS is also great because it has a certain 'fool proof' element. A CMS protects the layout integrity of the page. When content is edited, the underlying code remains hidden, and unable to be altered. This prevents simple updates from becoming layout disasters

- **Easily Access Scalable Feature Sets**

  Easily extend the functionality of your site. Most WCMS software includes plug-ins or modules that can be easily installed to do this

- **Maintain Web standards With Regular Upgrades**

  Active WCMS software usually receives regular updates that include new feature sets and keep the system up to web standards

A good content management system like Joomla will allow you to:

- Import and/or create documents and other digital content
- Identify all the key users and roles within the creation/maintenance of your site
- Define workflow tasks
- Keep each stakeholder aware of work being done on any content
- Track and manage multiple versions of an piece of content
- Alter your site presentation and layout via templates and add-ons to improve functionality

Get a Great Looking Website by Selecting a Sexy & Professional Joomla Template

Joomla is the most widely used open source CMS in the world. The key term here is that it is open source—it is freely available to everyone. In fact, so many people use Joomla that people actually make a living off of the various products and applications that you can add into your website (including great looking templates).

At *lead creation* we use two vendors that have some extremely functional and professional looking templates. One is Rocket Theme (http://www.rockettheme.com), which we personally find to be more professional and more functional than other templates as they use their own applications, but don't go too far so as to 'reinvent the wheel'. The other vendor that we like to use is YooTheme:

(http://www.yootheme.com). These templates seem a little more 'fun' and not as formal. The applications they use also require more knowledge and more involvement to make them function as intended.

Some content management systems force you to keep a certain design scheme, only allowing you to change the basic layout of elements and color choices. Our two recommendations offer you more flexibility and freedom. You can view these templates by following the links on these sites to 'live demo'. These act as live websites, so you are able to navigate around and make them function as they usually would.

What to Look For in a Great Template

When you first look at these templates, they may seem overly complex and full of confusing bits and pieces. These 'bits and pieces' add functional ability to a site. On the demo page, however, they include every single one, hence the clutter. It's important to know that you will only use 20% or 30% of these to improve functionality on any one page. Therefore your site, created from this template will not appear anywhere near so cluttered or confusing.

A website is made up of boxes within boxes. Each page is a box and within that box you will have your header (another box) and your menu (another box) and your content (another box) and your footer (another box). In templates each of these boxes are called 'modules'. You are able to choose to publish these modules in different positions on the page. The great thing about these templates is there is now no need to move these boxes around with messy HTML script. When you don't publish a certain module in a certain position then the other modules around it will shift and move to keep your site neat and clean.

You need to be looking at how these boxes are going to be presented on the page. If you have a menu down the left, then what will the content look like? Will you include another box at the top or at the bottom of the page? You need to use your mind's eye to conceptually view the website as you see it happening.

Whichever template you end up choosing, you will most likely have to play around with it for a little while until you work out what best suits your business. With a good CMS and professional template, you will have firsthand control over how your website looks and runs. Put in the time and effort to get it just right. Once you get the right one, when you want to add a page, all you have to do is go to your Joomla backend and click 'add new article' and it will be added in the same format as your existing template. So who needs an 'IT guy' anyway?!

Different Templates = Different Sites, So Experiment to Get it Right

Different templates will give your site a very different look and feel. At *lead creation* it took us a few goes to get our site right. Below is an example of http://www.leadcreation.com.au with two different templates – note the vast differences between them. The template plays a big role in how well your site will work, so make sure you get the right one or choose a new one if whatever you've gone with doesn't feel right.

www.leadcreation.com.au circa April 2009 – first template we tried:

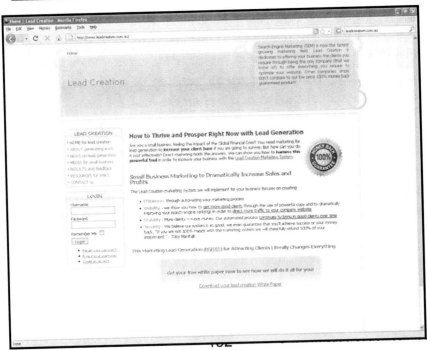

www.leadcreation.com.au October 2009 – the template we currently use looked like this before we tweaked the appearance:

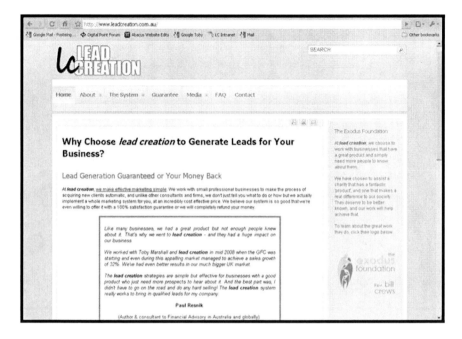

See the difference an alternate template can make!

Once you've finally chosen a template you're completely happy with, how can you make sure people (potential clients included) are able to find your website when they're searching for products and services like yours online? Read on to find out some quick and effective tips to make your site more visible. (And read the SEO chapter for even more hints!)

With a half days work by our in-house techo, you can see the difference made to this template, and as of October 2009 this is how our site looks:

Great Tips to Improve Your Website Traffic

So once you've set up your CMS, what can you do to increase the number of people visiting your site everyday?

Market & Promote Your Website with 8 Great Tips

Just because you get a website, it doesn't mean it'll immediately get flooded with expressions of interest in your business—*unless* you properly optimise and manage it. Here are eight simple tips to ensure you achieve the maximum visibility for your site.

1) Update your content regularly. Why not have a "what's new" or "upcoming events" section on your site and keep it updated with new content? On your homepage have a link to this page. This gives visitors a reason to come back more than once and it also attracts Google's programs to your site more often to determine relevancy and helps improve your ranking on their search results page.

2) Provide valuable information. If your site is an information resource, people will visit and revisit in order to learn. Rather than just acting as a brochure, your site will effectively be providing a useful service in and of itself. You can provide White Papers, tips, fact sheets, articles, 'how to' information and whatever else will be useful to your target market to attract them to your site. This will show that you are truly an expert in your field and also helps to initiate a positive, trusting relationship between your company and a potential client.

3) Have a free e-newsletter people can subscribe to. Create a short e-newsletter of content which is interesting and related to your industry which you can send to willing visitors. Add a personal touch to these e-newsletters, keep them friendly and informative, and this will help develop an ongoing relationship with potential clients and keep you fresh in their minds.

© www.leadcreation.com.au

4) Links: Link to good sites and ask them to link back to you. When other sites link to yours, more visitors will find you, and your ranking on the search results page will go up in Google. The simplest way to get more links is to ask! Email sites which have professional and valuable content and ask to link to them, and if they would link to your in return. Both parties benefit from this in SEO terms.

5) Add your webpage address to your automatic email signature. Send out your web address in every email, even personal ones. The more people who see your web address the more potential visitors you will have to your site.

6) Send a one-time announcement to everybody in your address book. Only do this once or you'll risk annoying people. Send a brief message telling everyone what you're doing and where your site is. You may even rekindle some long lost contacts.

7) Join one or two forums and post messages regularly - with your full signature. Join a forum that your target audience read and contribute valuable info regularly. Don't spam the sites or you could damage your reputation.

8) Put your website address on all of your print materials. For every invoice, business card, letter, brochure, newsletter, fax and so on and so on that you send out, don't lose the opportunity to promote your business. Include your web address on everything.

Too Busy for DIY? Have *lead creation* do it for you

Hopefully in this chapter we've provided an informative guide to getting started creating and managing your own website through a simple and comprehensive CMS like Joomla. It can take some time getting used to the software, choosing your template and uploading your content, but if you've got the time and inclination, this is an incredibly rewarding and cost-effective process.

However, if you'd rather direct your time and energy into other aspects of your business, this doesn't mean your only option is to hire an expensive web designer or programmer. *lead creation* has a great young team of designers and website professionals who can implement the processes we've described in this chapter for your benefit.

For our clients, we set up and teach you how to manage your own website using the Joomla Content Management system. In consultation with the client, we choose the best and most professional looking template for their specific needs. We can customise background colors, font colors, and some page colors depending on what the template will allow. We are also able to upload your graphics (logo etc) to the template so that your website looks like exactly that: **your website**.

By using this system, we ensure that you get a cheap yet professional website—and more than that we make sure it's properly optimized so that potential clients can actually find it. We make you a website guaranteed to increase traffic and sales, all by using the effective techniques described in this book. If you're interested in more information, please feel free to visit our website and contact us.

Remember to also read the SEO, copywriting and autoresponder chapters as well for website tips. Clearly all these topics are interrelated.

Chapter 7: Autoresponders— The Incredibly Cheap & Effective Way to Stay in Touch

What can an Autoresponder do for my Business?

At some point everyone's received the email 'John Smith is out of the office and will return at the end of the month.' This email was delivered by an autoresponder system (computer software program) which sends an automatic reply to whoever emails. But there's **a lot more** an autoresponder can do than simply informing your friends that you're out of the office. Did you know that an autoresponder is an incredibly effective tool for turning sales leads into clients?

Now, an autoresponder won't write emails for you. Nor is it used to spam people by sending unsolicited emails. An autoresponder system is useful because it allows you to set up a sequence of prewritten emails that are sent out to prospects in your database at regular intervals determined by you.

In order to do this, you need to capture details from people who visit your website. Usually, this is done by offering them a free White Paper, or something else such as a newsletter which they can only receive if they submit an email address first.

Besides sending out simple, standardised messages, autoresponders can also send out an unlimited number of follow-up messages that can be delivered at intervals over a certain period of time. Whether it's done through your email program or your web server, you are able to keep your client base, and prospective customers, informed and up-to-date with the goings on of your company. It's also a valuable tool in providing recipients with product and service information.

The point of using an autoresponder is that when people search for services like yours in Google, they may just be inquiring. They may not be ready to commit money at this stage. **An autoresponder allows you to:**

1. Keep in touch
2. Deliver information a potential client might value
3. Develop an ongoing relationship so that the client begins to trust you
4. Position your business as the expert in the field so that when potential clients are ready to commit, they come to your business first

Stay Front of Mind with Clients who aren't ready to buy just yet

Once you have a potential client's email address, you can send them a series of marketing emails in order to inform them of, and ultimately sell them your services. It is <u>crucial</u> that this information is relevant to what the potential client is seeking - you don't want to spam them because this will annoy them and turn them away from using your company in the future.

However, if you send subtle, engaging and informative content to a potential client through an autoresponder system, you will keep yourself front of mind. When they are ready to commit to using services like yours, they will think of you first.

It's Useful for more than the 'On Vacation' Emails

While it's really handy to let people know you're out of the office, there are much better ways to utilise autoresponse technology.

Effective Ways to Use an Autoresponder

1. Include autoresponder sign up forms on all the important pages of your website. Give them an incentive to sign up such as by offering them a free White Paper

2. Immediately acknowledge those who contact you. Let people know you've received their email and you'll get back to them shortly

3. Let those on your mailing list know you've added a new blog to your website

4. Send out an FAQ document that tackles the questions that are often asked about your product or service

5. Make all your company articles and newsletters accessible via autoresponder

6. Offer a sequence of free reports or online courses to position your company as the expert in the industry. Predetermine how often you'll send these

7. Offer chapters or excerpts from books or e-books you've created

8. Send subscribers any videos or audio related to your products or services

9. Send out a survey about your product to get valuable feedback

10. Recommend programs or products that your company is affiliated with

Why do I Need an Autoresponder?

A good autoresponder system will:

- Allow you numerous domains
- Work 24/7
- Notice if there are duplicate email addresses, and so will not send the same message more than once to an email
- Send only to working, confirmed emails
- Provide links which allow people to quickly unsubscribe if they choose
- Allow you to customise the content sent out so that you can include 'Hi Tom' (when you are actually sending to Tom!). Having everyone's names on their emails makes them look a little more like personal emails
- Easily allow you to create HTML emails even if you've never done so before
- Allow you to send plain text emails for when people have HTML turned off
- Show you whether any emails 'bounced' i.e. weren't received for whatever reason
- Will remove emails that bounce from your lists
- Let you have as many autoresponders as you want – one for a particular product, one for newsletters, one for follow up emails and so on and so on!
- Allow you to send as many emails in a sequence as you want
- Create and maintain as many lists as you want
- Collect an unlimited number of subscribers
- Collect proof that someone has subscribed to your list to receive emails from you if they ever forget they did and complain
- Allow you to have control over the management of your lists
- Let you search through your lists for particular people
- Let you preset dates you want certain emails sent out so that even if you're not in the office or near a computer that day, the email will still go out

The Upside of Email Marketing

Many small businesses aren't confident that 'email marketing' is a good idea. They think it will alienate potential clients and give them a bad reputation. This is a very common reaction and completely understandable when we think about the typical way most businesses practice it. And they're completely right. Just think, if you received numerous irrelevant and repetitive emails on a product or service that you weren't interested in, without any clear ways to unsubscribe and be left alone, you'd be annoyed too. That's spam.

There are ways you can use emails in a professional and effective way, to attract and retain clients instead of repelling and alienating them. Firstly, research shows that 31% of people like to be marketed to by email (although they don't mean spam like 'Viagra' sellers, of course).

Secondly, there is a fundamental truth of marketing:

> **There are lots of different marketing media:**
> Media stories (from PR); ads; brochures; emails; seminars; posted letters; newsletters and faxes and so on.

What worries businesses the most when emailing, is annoying their potential customers. And you certainly will if you frequently send people unsolicited junk without telling them how they can unsubscribe. In this situation, yes, email marketing is a terrible way to generate leads.

However, this can easily be avoided. As long as you create relevant content for your audience, keep your sales pitches subtle, don't send too often and always include an option to unsubscribe, you shouldn't alienate potential customers. A carefully created email *will* generate leads. For people who have subscribed to receive emails from *lead creation* clients, we implement our Auto Responder system using mailchimp.com to automatically send out a sequence of relevant emails, which include the option to unsubscribe everytime.

Rules You *Must* Follow When Emailing a Cold List

A 'cold list' is a list of people whose details you have, who you intend to market to, who have not expressly agreed to receive any material from you. For business-to-business marketing. In Australia, you are allowed to send unsolicited content if it is relevant to the reciever's business. However, it is a grey area where the bureaucrats err on the side of the receiver, so to avoid complaints, there are **three rules we strongly recommend our clients follow when emailing to a cold list:**

1. Never send more than **two** emails. In these emails you give them the opportunity to register to receive more information from you. If they haven't registered after the two emails, you take them off the email list. Permanently

2. The email must be carefully tailored to a small, very targeted list. A list for whom the offer of a free White Paper is likely to be seen as valuable if they read the email

3. You tell them in the second email that this is the second and last email they will be receiving from you (of course you still include the automatic unsubscribe button). This message goes near the top of the email

While we are careful about the marketing messages and content we send out in email, there is of course an overarching rule that we advise all our clients: **only** use email if you feel comfortable with it. It is a valuable but not critical component. Not sending any emails is not mission threatening, as it is a very small part of lead generation.

Start Utilising an Autoresponder Now!

You won't have any trouble finding a company who can offer you autoresponder services. While some companies provide the service for free, others offer it for a small fee (approximately $20 or $30 per month).

Some websites that offer autoresponder services include:

- mailchimp.com
- sendfree.com
- shoppingcart.com
- getresponse.com

Whichever autoresponder you choose, you'll receive instructions on how to set it up and transfer your text. We recommend Mail Chimp

Personalise your messages with a signature, your name, your company name and contact details. Keep the message brief, relevant, and informative. It's also a good idea to include a short personal message about your company and why you're the expert. It should be a subtle message, but still strong enough to sell your product or service.

Your Quick Guide to MailChimp

MailChimp is used to:

- Send HTML newsletters from templates
- Maintain email lists and groups
- Capture data through website forms
- Send follow up auto-responses to downloads
- Gather analytics on email performance and activity

At *lead creation* we use all of the above functions daily. Take advantage of them all to keep in contact with your clients and leads.

The setup of some MailChimp functions does take some IT knowledge, but there are quite user friendly visual designers for the purpose of designing new templates for your HTML emails as well as visual designers to create forms from which you can capture data and send downloads. Don't be deterred by the silly monkey and the colourful images—this software is extremely powerful and this company thoroughly understands marketing.

Intro to MailChimp

There are two different types of MailChimp accounts:

Free Accounts – This allows you a limited number of emails per month and will keep the MailChimp badge on all emails sent out. You are allowed up to 500 list members on this account.

Paid Accounts – Prices here vary by the amount of members in your list. You are allowed to send unlimited emails per month and are able to remove the MailChimp badge from your emails.

When you first start out with MailChimp there will be a few things that they will ask of you before you are able to fully use your account. They will ask that you import a list (they may also ask where you've got that list from so that they know you're not spamming) and then they will ask that you send a 'campaign' (HTML email) to that list.

Navigation

MailChimp navigation is quite easy once you get used to it. However, this can be challenging as there are a few sections and options that intuitively should be a submenu category or in the side menu, but aren't there.

Once you login to MailChimp you will be taken to your 'Dashboard' and see menus like this:

Each of these tabs should be used frequently. Their uses are as follows:

Dashboard – shows you an overview of your campaigns, tutorial videos and 'Chimp Chatter', which is a newsfeed of recent activity within MailChimp. The side menu here is where you can create new HTML email templates by clicking on my templates. An HTML email is an email with images, background color, logos and so on in it.

Campaigns – this tab is where you can create and send an HTML email to a predefined list.

Lists – this is where you manage your lists; these can be opt-in lists or not opt-in. You must be aware that there are very strong laws against spam. If someone has not opted into a list and they report you, you can be banned from using your domain, MailChimp and fined.

Within the lists tab you are able to manage your list settings, create signup form web pages, create signup forms to embed onto your website, create initial email replies to signups and control other tools. We will explore these functions later.

Reports – this is where you can view your list and campaign performance and compare performance to other campaigns. You are also able to view where in the email people have clicked and even link MailChimp with your Google Analytics account.

Autoresponders – to maintain an automated contact with the members of your list you should create an Autoresponder. These are preloaded emails that are designed to send emails to this list at different times after the opt-in. For instance, lead creation has set up 7 email newsletters to follow up with our opt-in process. These emails are sent to each person exactly 1 week, 2 weeks, 3 weeks and so on after they have signed in.

How to get your Emails Opened, Not Junked

The two most important factors to getting your emails opened are:

1) The From Line:

This needs to explain exactly who is sending the email. The name needs to be recognisable. Your company name will typically suffice. If you're sending to people who haven't registered to receive information from you, this may make them wary of opening, but if you use just any name, or your first and last name, you may make them far warier. After all, most people won't bother to open emails if they don't know the sender.

2) The Subject Line:

This needs to give the reader a compelling reason to open the email. It should be engaging, arouse curiosity, offer some promise of relevant, important information. The more personal and relevant it is to the person receiving it, the more likely they are to open it. It could have a time clause in it, to prompt the reader to act quickly and read now, not just to leave it and look at it later.

Curiosity is one of the main factors that drives people to open an email. One of the easiest ways to excite a recipient's curiosity is to start a sentence, then put an ellipsis and continue the sentence in the email body. These teasers can be very effective. An unfinished subject line creates great tension, making the reader want to find out the rest of the sentence and thus, open the message.

However, one small caution. A teaser subject line should be composed very carefully. If it looks too spammy, not only does it hurt your open rate, it can ruin the recipient's faith in you as a reputable marketer. With all that said, the best way to write a teaser subject line is to use implication. The Subject line should imply that the answer is in your email and tease the reader to open the message looking to find it.

There are certain words, however, that junk mail software will recognise and junk an email for. For example, **emails are likely to be marked as spam if:**

- The subject line contains the word "advertisement"
- The subject line contains "!" <u>AND</u> contains "$"
- The subject line contains "!" <u>AND</u> contains "free"
- The body copy contains the words "Guarantee" <u>AND</u> also contains "satisfaction" OR "absolute"
- The body copy contains the words "SPECIAL PROMOTION"
- **Learn others at:** http://office.microsoft.com/Assistance/9798/newfilters.aspx

So check your messages for any spam triggers—being shoved into junk mail won't get you any customers!

Chapter 8: Google AdWords— Cost-Effective Leads for Small Business

Business will never be the same again!

For 5 years I've wanted to use that headline, ever since my first Copywriting workshop! AdWords is the perfect opportunity.

It's a big claim, but that's how major the impact on business and particularly small business marketing is going to be. And it's already started to happen.

If small business advertising is being hit by the equivalent of a marketing tsunami, why have 95% of small businesses not noticed?

Before we answer that, some background for those of you who have been totally focused on your business and solving client problems...

What are Google AdWords?

When you search in Google, the results show up underneath the search box. Have you noticed that the results that come up on the right hand side or above these 'free listings' look different? These are 'Sponsored Links'—advertisements created with Google AdWords.

The name pretty much describes what AdWords do: people type in *words*, and the *ad* linked to those words appears. They are an incredibly effective and inexpensive method for small businesses to market online and to create and control a profitable flow of leads.

AdWords enables your site to show up on the first page of the search engine results for the words and phrases you know your potential clients will type into the search box to find your services. The best thing about AdWords is that *you don't waste a cent on ineffective marketing.* How is this possible? You only pay when people click on your ads.

AdWords are simply the ultimate in Direct Response Marketing, which as we showed in Chapter One is the only type of marketing that works for small business.

And yes, the other Search Engines like Yahoo also have AdWords. But it's like what happened in 1908 in America with the Model T Ford. The Tin Lizzie totally dominated the car market for everybody except the super rich. There was really only <u>one</u> car for Middle America, and of course it only came in black.

This is a <u>practical</u> book on small business marketing. We <u>only</u> want you to spend time and money in places that will help your business grow. Google is the Model T of today. Start with Google AdWords, and when you've got them working well and making you money, you <u>might</u> want to consider the others. If you have the time after servicing your new clients!

Why will Google AdWords change the world? And particularly the world of advertising small businesses?

Every person reading this book and virtually every knowledge worker goes to Google to start out research or to answer questions. And in particular, it's where most of us start our process of buying—what's out there? What does the service or product do? Where can I get it? What does it cost? Is there something cheaper or more effective? These are all questions we'll ask Google first.

AdWords are there when you begin your research process and as you refine it. And Google works hard and (usually) intelligently to deliver the right ads so the searcher finds the web pages they need. The Google mission is 'increasing relevance', and this is the bedrock of their amazing and growing dominance.

Why must AdWords become a key part of your advertising and of how you promote your small business?

Let's look at two alternative advertising approaches:

1. You pay a dollar or less when someone clicks on your ad—and less than 20 cents if you follow the advice in this chapter. Someone who's typed words into Google that match what you sell, and who has a good chance to be looking to buy from you.

<u>OR</u>

2. You pay a thousand dollars or ten thousand dollars to place an advertisement in a newspaper. Many thousands buy the paper, a few see your smallish ad (you're a small business; it's all you can afford). Most who see your ad ignore it as it's not relevant to them, or they are not ready to buy yet.

   Spending even a thousand dollars is a waste. Why? The two final nails in the coffin of mass media advertising are that

   1) it's not interactive, so they have to make a lot more effort to get in touch with you. Whereas it's only one click on Google. 2) Have you heard about the research on how few young people read newspapers? Who would want to be a publisher!

So, the Math:

   If the newspaper ad works really well, you'll get fifty qualified leads, and let's say it only cost a $1000 and you only ran it once (freakish results, you must write great ads!). The ad runs, lot of effort, campaign is now over.

However, on Google you might spend $50, or ideally $10, and also generate fifty leads. And you can keep testing and refining the ad campaign, reducing the costs. And the leads keep flowing, day by day. This campaign is ongoing and low cost.

Guess it falls in the no-brainer category. So why haven't AdWords become a tsunami yet?

Well firstly, it sort of has: Even in little Australia, Google's revenue was nearly a billion dollars last year (and the Aussie dollar is currently about 88 cents to the mighty Greenback). That is significant and dwarfs a lot of traditional media, and that's happening in other countries as well.

Secondly, there are some powerful industries linked to the world of mass media advertising that are continuing to sell what they do in the traditional ways. Publishers, TV networks, radio networks and of course traditional advertising agencies. These are big strong companies and they won't vanish overnight.

But you and your small business can ignore this battle: Right now, Google AdWords are like 'low hanging fruit'—ripe for the picking.

Two final questions before we show you how to get started:

Will the price of AdWords go up as millions more small businesses start to use them? Of course, AdWords are like an auction, you bid to be on page one. Should this deter you? No, because they are cheap now. And you don't really have a choice as your competitors will be there even if you choose not to be.

Secondly, is Google's dominance a concern? Absolutely. They are challenging Microsoft (Google Apps: the perfect business platform for SMEs, we use it and love it); challenging Amazon (with Google Books), initially in books sales and they have an incredible business advantage in this challenge. But why will they stop at books; they potentially have an advantage in selling <u>any</u> product.

And finally in dominating AdWords, Google operate in what economists call a 'natural monopoly'. And such monopolies are virtually impossible to challenge without another technology breakthrough. Or unless the market demands something different and Google doesn't feel it needs to address that: Henry Ford thought consumers wanting a choice of colors was ridiculous. He paid for that view.

But these issues are for Governments and the big boys to sort out. Right now your small business needs to jump on the bandwagon and get rolling...

Simply go to the Google AdWords site today and set up an account. Once you have created an AdWords account, you then start creating Campaigns, Adgroups and finally the advertisements themselves.

The Frustration of AdWords Eliminated

Google AdWords is a powerful tool for gaining business today, however, many people don't know how to use it correctly and so instead waste a lot of time and money on it without gaining many sales leads. It can be an extremely frustrating and expensive system to use if you don't know how to improve the rates at which people are clicking on your ads.

Believe it or not, this is a good thing for you. It means that, with a little help and a lot of testing, you can discover how to write effective Google AdWords ads while your competitors simply throw up their hands in despair and eventually throw in the towel. You'll be able to utilize a marketing platform that not many of your competitors took the time to master. This will give you an exclusive way to access your niche market of prospective clients.

Google AdWords *can* be a cost-effective way to market once you know how to use it properly. Learning from the mistakes and successes of others will put you miles ahead when you come to write your own ads.

So sit back, grab a pen to underline and discover what you can do to make your Google AdWords the most effective they can be.

Getting Started – Setting up a Google Account

To create a Google Account, click on the accounts link at the top of the Google home page.

Enter a current email address, and choose a password. Once you've finished registering, you'll receive a verification email; within the email there is link that completes the verification process. You will need to follow through the rest of the steps as Google prompts you – setting your currency and so forth. Once you have your Google Account open, do a search for Google AdWords and sign up for an account in the same way.

Google also provides useful detailed guides to help you get used to navigating the AdWords system. Note that you will also get access to the extremely valuable Google Analytics program when you set up your Google Account.

When creating an account, keep these guidelines in mind:

- Your Google Account username should be an email address from which you currently send and receive mail, unless you'd prefer to sign up for Gmail
- Your password should be at least eight characters long and can't be a commonly used word. Select a unique combination of letters and numbers
- In the Word Verification section, you'll need to type the wavy characters exactly as they appear in the picture
- Creating a Google Account doesn't give you Gmail
- Signing up with a Gmail account will lock you into that email for life. You cannot change your email later.

Understanding Googlespeak

To write a Google AdWords ad, you need to understand the basic terminology and structure of this advertising medium. **The Key Terms:**

Ads are the actual advertisements you want to show on Google. You can create one or more Ads and put these in an adgroup.

An **adgroup** allows you to group one or more ads together and display these in rotation when the adgroup's keywords are typed into Google. Each adgroup can have a maximum Cost-Per-Click (CPC) set for it, as well as CPC per keyword. You would normally have an adgroup for each individual product or service you are advertising, or for specific groups of related keywords.

The **Keywords** you choose for a given adgroup are used to target your ads to potential customers. For example you may be an accounting firm, and so your keywords might be 'accountant', 'accounting', 'tax accountants', 'Sydney accountants' and so on – whatever potential clients are likely to type into Google to find products and services like yours. (Read the chapter on keywords if you haven't already to find out more about discovering the best keywords for your business). Keep in mind that the longer your key phrases become, the cheaper the bid prices become and the more likely you will be targeting one of your potential clients.

The **Cost-Per-Click (CPC)** is the pricing structure used by some online channels to charge an advertiser each time a user clicks on the advertiser's ad. The amount is usually set by the advertiser, not by the channel. Prices typically range from 9 cents to over ten dollars per click. This is an ideal method of payment for advertisers who need to guarantee they only pay for those viewers of the ad that click on it and visit a page on their site. You are able to completely control your cost and bid price.

A **Campaign** consists of one or more adgroups, and allows you to set a budget on the total spend, as well as letting you target the adgroups (and therefore Ads) to specific Sites, Languages, Countries, Cities, and even to a specific local area (for example, a 30 mile radius around your business location).

Ad Copy are the words that 'prepare the deal', that get people to click and then go to your site. To avoid any confusion: Ads don't sell; they just warm-up the customer-to-be. They ask for clicks.

Your **Quality Score** is the basis for measuring the quality and relevance of your ads and determining your minimum CPC bid for Google and the search network. This score is determined by your keyword's clickthrough rate (CTR) on Google, and the relevance of your ad text, keyword, and landing page. You <u>can</u> control your score. By following the rules later in this chapter—put simply, a high score means you pay less for your ads.

Your **Landing Page** is the web page where customers will 'land' when they click your ad. The web address for this page is often called a 'destination URL' or 'clickthrough URL.'

Understanding Quality Score

Quality Score

Quality Score is the crux of every keyword used in Google AdWords. Every keyword is ranked using this score (on a scale of 1 to 10) to measure how relevant your keyword is to your overall campaign. The position of your ad is directly related to your Quality Score plus your Bid Price. Hence, the better your quality score, the less you have to bid to appear higher up the rankings.

While Quality Score formulas for AdWords are constantly changing, the core components remain more or less the same:

- The historical clickthrough rate (CTR) of the keyword and the matched ad on Google
- Your account history, which is measured by the CTR of all the ads and keywords in your account
- The historical CTR of the display URLs in the ad group
- The quality of your landing page
- The relevance of the keyword to the ads in its ad group
- The relevance of the keyword and the matched ad to the search query
- Your account's performance in the geographical region where the ad will be shown

In basic terms, your landing pages should be loaded with the keywords you are bidding on, you should maintain a click thru rate for all campaigns above around 0.7% and you should keep your ads highly relevant to the keywords that have triggered them to be displayed.

Different Forms of Keywords

There are 3 different forms of keywords:

Broad Match – Broad match keywords are very indefinite. Examples of how a broad match keyword is written would be:

> dog training guide
> train my dog
> ways to train a dog

Search terms that could potentially trigger these keywords would be:

> training a guide dog
> my dog and i caught a train

ways a dog could hurt itself

As you can see, the words in the keyword don't have to appear in the search term in any relevant order, and not all of the words necessarily have to appear. We suggest that you do not use broad matching.

Phrase Match – Phrase match keywords are more precise. They are the best terms to use. Examples of how a phrase match keyword is written would be:

> "dog training guide"
> "train my dog"
> "ways to train a dog"

Search terms that could potentially trigger these keywords accordingly would be:

> buy a dog training guide
> new ways to train my dog
> ways to train a dog to not bark

As you can see, all words within the quotations must appear in the search term in the order that they are written. There may be other words surrounding your phrase. We strongly suggest that you use phrase matching.

Exact Match – The search terms that trigger exact match keywords must be exactly as the keyword is written, just like a phrase match, but without any other words appearing either side of the phrase. You may use exact match, but the traffic will be low. Exact match keywords are also generally much cheaper than any other keywords. Examples of how you would write an exact match are:

> [dog training guide]
> [train my dog]
> [ways to train a dog]

AdWords Format – Learning the Rules of the Game

An ad written for Google AdWords has a very specific format. You are very limited to the maximum number of characters you can use (including spaces and punctuation), so use them wisely. An AdWords ad looks like this:

<u>Expert Home Loan Comparisons</u>	**25 characters inc. spaces max**
Obtain The Best Advice On Fees	**35 characters inc. spaces max**
Minimise Monthly Payments With Us!	**35 characters inc. spaces max**
www.YourDomainName.com.au	**35 characters inc. spaces max**

As you can see, an AdWords ad has:

- 4 rows per ad (of which, one is the destination URL – the page they are being sent to)
- No pictures
- No colours except for blue for the headline and green for the URL – Google does this automatically and you can't change it
- Punctuation marks only in the body copy and NOT the heading

How to Write a Good Google Ad

There are a number of diverse factors that determine how successful an ad will be.

A good ad is:
- Relevant to your target audience
- Clear and direct
- Interesting and engaging, arousing curiosity
- Able to make people want to act right now
- And, most importantly, has the keywords that they are searching for in the ad (and the same keywords must be on the landing page too.) **HOT TIP: Never send them to your home page!**

Probably the most important element of your ad is the **headline**. The headline is what people read first and often the only thing they'll read if it doesn't grab and hold their attention. One way to make sure your headline jumps out at potential clients is to use keywords in it. If a person typed in the word 'accountant' and their local area and your ad had those two keywords in its headline, your ad would obviously be extremely relevant to that person and would hold their attention. You need to work out what your clients are searching for and use those specific terms in your ad.

Apart from the headline, it's important when writing one of these ads to consider your tone. Pick the tone that best suits your audience. You want to demonstrate that you 'speak the same language' as your potential customer. Clear and simple is often the most effective ad copy to use. Aim to make your ads personalised and ensure that ad titles and/or the body copy match (or come close to matching) the keywords that were typed in to bring the page up.

Six Simple Steps to Write Amazing AdWords Easily

Even if you do nothing else, make sure you use the following simple, easy, fool proof and 'sure-fire' techniques to create your ads. You *will* reap the benefits:

1. **Include keywords in your ad**

2. **Include phrases that relate to your keywords**

3. **Be as specific as you can (e.g. specify the city or region you serve)**

4. **Stand apart through benefits, not through tricks and gimmicks**

5. **Think of your URL as part of the ad**

6. Use common words, plain and simple words

Quick Tips:

Tip 1: Ensure the Ad has a specific amount of chosen keywords that will trigger your Google ad word to be displayed in the sponsored links.

Tip 2: The body copy should have keywords included in them as they will be highlighted/bolded if the keyword is searched for. Why? Because the more bolded print a customer or searcher sees, the more your Ads are inline with what they are searching for. Every ad you create should have a minimum of 4 keywords in the ad itself.

Tip 3: There should be a keyword in the title of the Google ad word ad along with 3 other keywords in the body copy of the ad. Keep this in mind when creating URLs, registering domains, creating sub domains and creating domain extensions etc. because if your have a domain name with which you are able to utilise an important keyword, the relevancy of the site would be deemed higher and your quality score higher, so you pay less.

Six Rules for Better AdWords Copy –Explained

In order to write good, effective ads that get people to click through AND have a good conversion rate when they get to your page, you need to make sure you do the following. (Each of these is explained in further detail below):

1. **Match the user's query as closely as possible**

2. **Send appropriate cues by speaking the same language your target customer speaks**

3. Filter out inappropriate prospects

4. Get the prospect's "action motor" going by inserting a "call to action"

5. Based on CTR and conversion data, pick the winning Ads among several you've been testing. Occasionally, introduce new Ads so the testing process never stops—you keep 'split testing'.

6. Inject some flair or brand appeal in the process

Rule #1: Match Ad Titles to Searched Keywords

For example, if a user was searching for "Emerald Jewellery", an ad that may be triggered could be:

Emerald Jewellery Store
Earrings, Bracelets, Watches & More
Check Out Our Weekly Specials!
www.EmeraldJewellery.com.au

HOWEVER, this ad is fine if the user was just looking for emerald jewellery in general, but what if the search query had been "Emerald Bracelets"? It would have been beaten by a more specific ad run by a competitor. So, in order to improve the performance of this ad, it needs to be more targeted:

Designer Emerald Bracelets
Emerald Bracelets By Top Designers
Dazzling One-Of-A-Kind Items!
www.EmeraldJewellery.com.au

Targeting of an ad is key. So within the adgroup, there should be multiple Ads that targets the different pieces of jewellery e.g. necklaces, rings, anklets etc. This utilises the keywords you have added to your campaign.

Rule #2: Send Appropriate Cues to Your Target Audience

Speak the language of the prospective client. From the example above "one-of-a-kind" may attract customers who prefer to have unique pieces of jewellery and you may have hit home in "speaking their language".

Rule #3: Filter Out People Unlikely to be Potential Clients

This is done by keyword selection and targeted phrasing. Keywords must not be broad (so that your ad shows up in irrelevant searches) e.g. if you are offering loans for homes and the title is "Low Interest Loans", you will get people looking for personal loans, student loans, car loans etc. By adding the word "home" e.g. "Low Interest Home Loans", you can eliminate a large percentage of non-productive clicks.

Rule #4: Include a 'Call to Action'

In plain English, that means put an action word/verb into the ad copy which compels the user to want to take an action.
For example:

> Need Property Advice?
> Call Our Property Advisers Today!
> Get the Best Home Loan with Low Fees
> www.FinancialPlanner.com.au

The "Call Our Property Advisers Today" is intended to compel users to act upon the suggestion and seek advice.

Rule #5: Run a Test, Keep the Winning Ads

Have different variations of an ad copy and run tests to see which garners the best response, sales and leads. Don't over do this by writing numerous Ads. Standard is 3 Ads per adgroup each being shown an equal amount of time and randomly rotated so they all get an equal time to 'sell'. If one ad is a clear winner, create two variations of it, and test these three together. And keep going until you run out of variations and have a standout ad.

Rule #6: Inject Some Flair

This is tweaking the tone, language and wording of the ad and this technique depends heavily on the audience. This may not work well with the wider audience.

Sell a solution, not a Service or Product. For example, if you sell Acne Cream you could have the term in your title. But you could also try "Acne Problems" and use "acne cream" in the body copy.

Quick Start Methods to Writing AdWords ASAP

When you're writing your ad and don't quite know where to start, why not try to write a version of the ad for each of the following styles. You can include these in the same adgroup and see what works best. Different approaches send a different message and different ones may appeal to your target audience for different reasons. It's your job to work out which approaches/messages work best for your niche market and to capitalise on them!

The different 'quick start' styles are as follows:

1) The Benefit & Feature Tactic:

Line 1 benefit	-	What benefits the users' emotion
Line 2 feature	-	something specific about the offer

2) The Negative Sale Ad:

Use scare tactics -   e.g.: don't get scammed buying 'adware'

3) The Hype Selling Tactic:

Make it sound too good to be true

4) The Controversy Angle:

Say something bad about the industry or competitors - e.g. Stop using diet pills now and find out what really works

5) Copying Your Competitors:

Examine competitors Ads and use similar techniques - don't just use it word for word. See what they're doing and think about how you could make this better for your products and services

6) Use a Review style:

Sound like an expert in the industry, compare and review sites or products

7) Ask a Question:

E.g. "Need to lose Weight? Find the most effective diet pills"

Small Business Marketing with a Cost-Effective AdWords Strategy

Google AdWords is an effective method of quickly getting well-targeted traffic to your website. We at *lead creation* utilise a proven technique called the 'long tail' keywords strategy - which means we advertise on often quite long phrases that not many other firms target. When people type these longer phrases into search engines like Google, it is more likely that they are seriously searching for a service like yours. And at 9 to 50 cents per ad, using Google AdWords is a very cheap way to increase the amount of traffic to your website.

Here are some of *lead creation*'s own ads just to demonstrate how the principles we've been talking about can be put into action. Our keyword for the following group was 'internet marketing strategies'. This is a 'long tail' keyword.

Ad 1:

Marketing On The Internet	**25 characters inc. spaces max**
Get Best Advice on Online Marketing	**35 characters inc. spaces max**
Generate Real Leads Fast: Free Info	**35 characters inc. spaces max**
www.LeadCreation.com.au	**23 out of 35 max characters inc. spaces**

Ad 2:

Easy Internet Marketing!	**24 out of 25 characters inc. spaces max**
Internet Marketing Can be So Simple	**35 characters inc. spaces max**
With Online Marketing Strategies	**32 out of 35 max characters inc. spaces**
www.LeadCreation.com.au	**23 out of 35 max characters inc. spaces**

Ad 3:

E-Marketing Too Tough?	**22 out of 25 characters inc. spaces max**
Best Internet Marketing Strategies	**34 out of 35 max characters inc. spaces**
For Small Businesses: Free Info Now	**35 characters inc. spaces max**

www.LeadCreation.com.au   **23 out of 35 max characters inc. spaces**

For the keyword 'lead generation' here were some more ad variations. Hopefully these examples will give you an idea of what you can do with your own ads.

Ad 1:

Online Lead Generation   **22 out of 25 characters inc. spaces max**

Create New Sales Leads Easily!   **30 out of 35 max characters inc. spaces**

Download Our Free White Paper Today   **35 characters inc. spaces max**

www.LeadCreation.com.au   **23 out of 35 max characters inc. spaces**

Ad 2:

Generate Leads Online   **21 out of 25 characters inc. spaces max**

Online Leads Are Waiting for You   **32 out of 35 max characters inc. spaces**

Lead Generation Made Easy At Last   **33 out of 35 max characters inc. spaces**

www.LeadCreation.com.au   **23 out of 35 max characters inc. spaces**

Ad 3:

Want More Sales Leads?   **21 out of 25 characters inc. spaces max**

Generate Leads Online-It's So Easy!   **35 characters inc. spaces max**

Find Out How Today: Free Download   **33 out of 35 max characters**

www.LeadCreation.com.au   **23 out of 35 max characters inc. spaces**

You can see how variations on the same keyword can generate different types of ads. You need to test different ads which make use of the same keyword against each other and work out which is best.

© www.leadcreation.com.au

Testing Your Ads – Survival of the Fittest

Once you find the most effective of your ads – with the highest click through rate **AND** conversion rate, this becomes your 'control' ad. The next step is that you need to tweak the ad somehow – change the word order, change the punctuation or some other small element – and test that against your control.

This is called 'split testing' or just testing. The aim is to find an ad which beats the best ad you have so far. You do this by testing different variations against it and seeing which achieves better results. This also allows you to see what elements of an ad simply 'kill it' in terms of reducing clicks through and conversions. You can then avoid these mistakes in the future.

As soon as you have an ad which outsells your control ad, the new ad replaces it and becomes your control. You then tweak again or devise completely new ads to compete against this one and replace it again as soon as you discover a better performer. This is an ongoing process which allows you to judge through measurable results which ads are the best ones to get you new sales leads.

Tips for Better AdWords

Keep your Keywords Focused

Group Keywords into tightly focused groups, and create an adgroup for each keyword grouping. This ensures that the Ads you create are extremely relevant to each adgroup, increasing your Click Through Rate (CTR). Don't write a generic Ad for all keywords. The best way to do this is to have multiple adgroups for your different set of keywords so that you can easily write specific Ads for each Group.

Use Keywords in Your Ads

Google highlights keywords found in search results - which includes the AdWords Ads, so if you use keywords in your Ads, then this will draw attention to your ad, increasing CTR.

Think About Where You Want Your Visitors to Arrive

Don't just send people to your homepage. If the information relevant to the ad they clicked on is not on that page, many will simply hit the back button on their browser, resulting in a wasted click charge to you. AdWords allows you to display your homepage URL whilst sending visitors to another page (i.e. The Landing Page), so choose the most relevant page on your site.

Your landing page should include the relevant keywords that you have bid on. Therefore, each of your Ads should have its own relevant landing page with relevant keywords you have optimized for.

Use Negative Keywords

When researching your keywords, be sure to eliminate any irrelevant searches by using negative keywords.

For example, for the keyword 'golf equipment', you should choose to add negative keywords for '-volkswagen' and '-vw'.

The Do's of Google AdWords:

- Pay attention to grammar, spelling and punctuation
- Adhere to Google's content policy (or the Ads will never see the light of day)
- Use words that target potential customers – you don't want people to click the ad and not purchase
- Be clear and unambiguous
- Have a convincing Landing Page (LP) as it will do all the selling. Make the ad relate to the LP
- The ad must cater to the user's/buyer's wants, needs and/or expectations immediately or else they will move on to the next vendor who is capable of doing so
- The Ads must be relevant enough to induce action, but specific enough to limit that action to potential customers only
- Have a clear, concise benefit statement, a value proposition, or third party endorsement
- Have a call to action
- Have an offer
- Have special wording that might weed out inappropriate prospects

The Don'ts of Google AdWords:

- Use abbreviations, acronyms and other devices that the target customer may not recognise. However, if target customer is familiar with them and they are relevant, use them, but ensure they are appropriate for the intended audience
- Copy a competitor's ad word for word – it makes your ad insignificant. You want your ad to stand out
- Not identifying the unique aspects of your product or service

- **Not using enough keywords or targeted words**
- **Sending people who click straight to your homepage rather than a targeted landing page specifically about what your ad spoke about**
- **Not testing different variations of ads or tracking results to find out what is working the best**
- **Not targeting your ad to a niche market only – 'everyone' is too broad to be your target market**

When In Doubt Try, Try Again

Google AdWords success may come from a wide variety of factors. **So why not try some of the following to spice up your ads:**

- ➢ Use keywords in your headline
- ➢ Use keywords in your body copy
- ➢ Use keywords in your URL
- ➢ Only have a small number of keywords for each adgroup
- ➢ Use targeted keywords – e.g. if you sell jewellery, you could use the words bracelet, ring, necklace, pendant and so on, or you could use the names of types of stones, the style of the piece or stone cut, or of the material the jewellery is made of. Think of what words specifically your potential clients may type in and use these in your ads
- ➢ Address only your target market – if you sell something for women, include a call out to ladies in your ad to make sure men aren't clicking onto your ad
- ➢ Use plain or conversational English
- ➢ Ask a probing question that arouses curiosity or interest
- ➢ Include a guarantee
- ➢ Include a specific price

- ➢ Offer instructions (read, download) or 'How to' or a 'Guide to'

- ➢ Use any of the words: Secrets, Discover, The Key to, How to, Free, You, Tips, Today, Now, You need to, Changes, Download, Exposed

- ➢ Don't use the word 'buy'

- ➢ Don't include your company name in the headline if you are a small business. If you were Qantas or Target or Myer or a big well-known company, only then might it be beneficial

- ➢ Promote the benefits of your product or service in your ad – it won an award, it is simple and easy, it is cost-effective, an industry expert recommended it, it has measurable results, use industry jargon, savings – use proof that what you're selling works and is valuable to make your ad compelling

- ➢ Capitalise your keywords but don't capitalise small words like 'and', 'to', 'is' and so on

- ➢ Don't repeat yourself in the ad – don't use the same phrase keyword twice in one ad

- ➢ Use emotional words in your ad

- ➢ Try using rhyme, rhythm, alliteration, puns – make the language fun

- ➢ Try different kinds of punctuation – does a . work better than a ! or a ? Why not use an ellipsis (three dots) at the end of your sentence to increase curiosity? It tells people that once they click there is more information waiting on the other side …

- ➢ Make sure the URL brings up a page directly related to your ad

- ➢ Sometimes it works to use incorrect grammar or 'edgy' sentences where words are left out. Experiment and see what works better for you – perfect English or a little bit of imperfect English. (Don't go too crazy though.) E.g. you might use 'is' instead of 'are' in an ad

- ➢ Use variations on the same ad –change the capitalisation, remove words like 'a, the, and, is, of' and so on, change the word order–and see what works best

➢ You'd be surprised what works sometimes so test even the smallest ad variations – change only one aspect at a time so you can see what's really making the difference

➢ Search your own keyword in Google and see what your competitors are doing

➢ Use a testimonial in your ad

➢ Include a time limit in your ad – For today only, limited to first twenty click-throughs

➢ Tell a story in your ad – How Mr Smith made $10K in a week...

What is Your Quality Score?

Google defines Quality Score as "the basis for measuring the quality and relevance of your ads and determining your minimum CPC bid for Google and the search network. This score is determined by your keyword's click through rate (CTR) on Google, and the relevance of your ad text, keyword, and landing page."

Poor quality scores are often caused by:
- Having too many different types of keywords in one adgroup
- Too many different adgroups pointing to one landing page
- Thin (or not easily visible) content
- Bidding on keywords which have a history of low relevance ads
- Ads, landing pages and keywords which Google regards as not being closely related to each other

You can solve poor quality score problems and improve your score by:
- Splitting the keywords in your adgroups into smaller groups, and sending underperforming keywords into their own adgroups (so they do not drag down the Quality Scores of otherwise good keywords in good adgroups)

- Better targeted landing pages (ideally, keyword specific landing pages)
- Creating fresh new content for your site (i.e. – articles, blog posts, back issues of newsletters etc), and ensuring the content is easily visible using good internal navigation, or a site-map
- Getting rid of bad keywords
- And ensuring that your ads, keywords and landing pages are all closely related and relevant to each other

lead creation can do Your AdWords Campaigns

You can use an AdWords campaign to generate leads at any stage of your marketing. A web page isn't even required from you to get started—Google will assist you in creating one for this purpose and they won't charge you.

lead creation create campaigns for our clients to get high quality scores for all our ads as these will lead to much lower costs per click and a higher click through rate. This is complicated work but absolutely vital to an effective small business marketing strategy.

For *lead creation* clients, we make use of this fast growing, cost effective and powerful marketing media by setting up a maximum of five adgroups, each targeting different master keywords. Each adgroup will lead to a page on your website where you capture potential client information by offering them the gift of a White Paper that is relevant to what they were searching for. This will allow you to market to them automatically through the use of an autoresponder.

An AdWords campaign is likely to be but a small advertising cost, given that there is relatively low traffic on most of the keywords we will be using. The benefit of using 'long tail' keywords when people type them in it means they're serious and are more likely to buy from you.

Chapter 9: Social Networking —It Can Do Amazing Things for Your Small Business

What is Social Networking & Why Should I Care?

Think of Social Networking as like owning your own electronic newspaper. Your own electronic <u>niche</u> 'newspaper'. A paper where you do all the jobs.

As the *Distribution Manager*, you decide who you want to receive your newspaper. You also control which distribution <u>media</u> you choose to get your paper to it's readers—but it's all the same words, just on different media (with social networking the media is endless: LinkedIn, Twitter, blogging, YouTube, Delicious, Plaxo, and another page full of names!). As the *Editor*, you have the final say in what your audience gets to read, listen to or watch. As the *Journalist*, you do the research and decide what stories you will write. And the Editor can of course hire other journalists (writers).

And as the *Finance Director* you decide how much time and money you should spend to make your newspaper profitable. How much to spend to generate leads and raise the profile of your small business.

Now this is a book about lead generation for small business, for SMEs. **In this book we don't care about the social aspects of 'Social' Networking.** Care zilch about getting more friends and spending hours 'chatting' online—if you need more friends, the bookshops are overloaded with books on how to find them!

Our whole approach in this book on small business marketing is about first defining your niche. Your gold clients. The ones you want more of. It's all about <u>business</u> networking.

Well, **knowing your niche is absolutely fundamental to Social Networking**. How else can you create a 'newspaper' of value? Can you write content for everybody? If you did, would they be interested? No! More importantly, how can you select who to send it to? How can you build a distribution list?

If you don't have a niche, you might as well stand in 5th Avenue in New York or George St in Sydney with a loudspeaker, calling people to gather around you. And then try and collect all their business cards. Useless.

Our approach is simple and practical: Decide where you want more connections, where you want more clients for your small business. Then go out and connect to them following the strategies in this chapter.

Before we explore social (i.e. business) networking in more detail…

What Came Before Social Networking and Twits?

Before Twitter and LinkedIn, there was Networking—and it helps to refresh ourselves on the fundamental rules of networking <u>offline</u>. Why? Because people are people and the principles of networking haven't changed just because you're doing it on the internet. And the techniques are innate to humans and the communities they gather in. Whether in Karachi or San Fran.

In a nutshell, networking is about making a connection and establishing a relationship.

Networking 101 – The Basics You Need to Know

When we talk about how to build connections and networks, there are three vital concepts to keep in mind:

1. **You have to give people a reason to want you in their network**

   There are billions of people in the world, and as individuals we all have control over who we let into <u>our</u> network. Unless you can find a way to help the people you want to network with—a way that makes sense and is valuable to them—quite simply, they won't want you in their network. The network that <u>they</u> have complete power over!

   The aim is to give before you receive. As such, some networks have clichéd mottos like "Givers gain" but it is founded in truth. Now there are exceptions to this rule, primarily for the super rich, the very powerful or the very beautiful. But you could argue that they are 'giving' their beauty or sharing their power. However, this is for 1% of the world: you run a small business, you want to promote your small business and you're not super rich (yet!)

   This first step is absolutely vital. It is the foundation stone. Give Now. Receive later.

2. **People have to know you, and what you're good at**

   This is the second foundation stone of networking theory. It's not just about going to a conference or networking group and meeting and chatting with people. It's about making sure others know what <u>you</u> are good at. There are critical things you need your networking colleagues to know about your small business: What kind of clients can you really help? Why should they refer your services?

Remember the old cliché?

'It's not what you know, it's who you know' – it's rubbish!

It's who knows <u>you</u> and what you're good at

3. **Focus**

Work out which types (or groups) of people would be the most valuable for you to network with. Think about who else directly or indirectly influences or sells to the people you want to influence. Where do they congregate? How can you help *them*?

If your networking colleagues in the industry have this information about you, the next time their boss says: "We need a new financial advisor for our business", they'll put you forward. Referrals from inside a company—magic!

The Power of People You Barely Know

Many people know how important friends are in helping you find a new clients or a new job. However, when asked *which* friends are the most valuable, nearly all answer 'close friends and family'. But this just isn't the case. Your close friends are mostly not the best ambassadors for you anyway. They will be seen to be biased, and can also be too close to you to be objective.

Your close friends also tend to know the same people as you so they hear of the same marketing opportunities. *Loose* connections are the most beneficial—that is, those who by definition, move in different circles to you. There are also a lot more of them. When you are actively seeking new clients you should find ways to stay in touch with this broader circle—and ideally find ways to help them. To give.

Final comments on using friends to find new clients:

Your friends may never know what your ideal client looks like. It is human nature to assume our friends know: but they don't in nearly every case. Test this on ten friends—it would be highly unusual if you didn't get at least 5 different answers to this question.

Your 'How-To' Guide to Social Networking

Social networking is about bringing people together and it has many business applications. Particularly in generating leads for small business—it is just one more form of internet marketing, and increasingly becoming the most important.

By creating a profile on a major social networking site, adding people and having them add you, you can use this media as a way of staying in contact with existing clients and also to generate leads. It's also great for optimizing your website so you rank more highly on Google and become more visible online.

Most importantly: SMEs and small businesses can build a high profile in this new media at a price they can afford. Particularly the early adopters as there is currently so little competition from other small businesses as nearly all see it as new and scary.

Old Media vs. New Media

Twenty-first century customers are a breed unlike any seen before. They are increasingly tech-savvy, willing to do their own research to compare competing businesses, and are better able to see through manipulative marketing strategies. They have opinions to voice, value two-way communication, and no longer passively accept information presented to them, least of all by marketers. The days of 'Tell and Sell' are over—or soon will be.

It is no longer economically feasible to rely solely on old media such as print, TV and radio, even for large corporations. To reach today's consumers, marketers need to familiarise themselves with new media—blogging, 'tweeting' (aka microblogging), and social networks for professionals, such as LinkedIn. Advertising using old media such as newspapers, magazines, TV and radio is expensive and remains totally inappropriate for 99% of small businesses and SMEs (despite what the hard selling media salesmen say).

Today's marketing strategies must focus on informing, educating and raising awareness among potential customers. Old media has become transparent to the point of being inappropriate for reaching intelligent, discriminating consumers. Customers distrust marketers, but are willing to trust people —you must engage and interact with potential customers on a personal level. What better way to achieve this than by leaving your mark on social networks to enhance your company's image?

Why Use Social Media?—To Improve Your SEO!

Google's search engine has an 'I'm Feeling Lucky' button which bypasses the search results page to take you directly to the first site on the list. This means Google can be used to take your potential customers directly to your company's website. How? <u>Through a combination of search engine optimization and social networking.</u>

Creating links and backlinks from popular social sites such as LinkedIn and Twitter will direct traffic to your site, boosting your search engine ranking. Leaving your company or brand's mark on a social networking site will complement your search-engine optimization strategy and enhance your overall web presence.

What Social Networks Should You Use?

There are different types of social networking sites. **Facebook** is the main one that many people use or know of and is mainly for the young (and the restless!). **LinkedIn** is the business equivalent and is used by companies and business professionals to create networks of their peers.

There are many other networking sites, in fact too many to list here, and the list will be different if you are reading this in January 2010. And different again in June.

For marketing and other business purposes we recommend you use:

1. Blogging

2. LinkedIn

3. Twitter

Note that this ranking of the importance of social networking sites for business may change, and change rapidly. At the time of writing this chapter (mid October 2009) some research suggests that Twitter growth may be stalling. While for the last three months, LinkedIn has boomed. In fact, we now think that if you only did one thing on the Networks, it should be LinkedIn, and your blog comes second.

This book as you've no doubt gathered is all about lead generation for small businesses—and the more active the social networking site, the more it achieves this goal. So recently we have put a lot more emphasis on LinkedIn in the marketing we do for clients. And, of course, in our own marketing.

Different social networks attract different people. Using more than one social media _theoretically_ allows you to reach a greater number of potential customers, as well as a more diverse group of individuals. However, our most critical advice is to start with just one network and get it working for you—don't spread your resources too thinly. Note this is the same core message I delivered in more than 60 networking seminars and workshops I've run on how to build business networks in the days before LinkedIn, etc.

Commit to one group or network and get involved—and for SMEs and small businesses, there is no doubt that starting with LinkedIn gives

you the biggest bang for your buck. Particularly if you work in some form of professional services.

Businesses have been slow to utilise the low-cost or free opportunities provided by social networking in generating leads and increasing brand awareness. Social media marketing allows you to reach potential clients in an arena where a lot of your competitors aren't marketing because they just don't get it. In this chapter, you'll learn the ins and outs of using social media strategies to improve the marketing of your small business and get more clients.

Blogs

What is 'Blogging'?

Firstly, let's look at the traditional or common view of what blogging is:

A blog, originally short for "web log", is an online journal, where entries are available for anybody to read. Blogs are the perfect marketing tool, as they are widely used to vent opinions and ideas. Best of all, they are **free and easy** to set up and maintain.

From Blogger.com, here is the accepted definition of a blog:

> *"A blog is a personal diary. A daily pulpit. A collaborative space. A political soapbox. A breaking-news outlet. A collection of links. Your own private thoughts. Memos to the world. Blogs have reshaped the web, impacted politics, shaken up journalism, and enabled millions of people to have a voice and connect with others."*

Rubbish! Irrelevant!

That's the standard definition which applies to people who want to be <u>real</u> bloggers. It's highly unlikely that that is what you want to be. You have a business to run.

If you're in business this definition is irrelevant, in fact it's misleading. From the perspective of generating new clients, of small business marketing, **the main objective of blogging is to increase your web presence and direct traffic to your main website.** Nothing to do with news or giving politics a shake! Just business.

Blogs make people aware of the products and services you have to offer, and familiarise potential customers with your company or brand.

The secondary objective is to demonstrate your expertise and knowledge to your Gold Niche. You must of course have defined your 'inch wide, mile deep' gold niche <u>before</u> you even consider any social networking—or how will you know who you want to network with?!

Blogging in the traditional sense involves interacting within an online community. Remember, social networking and Web 2.5 is a two-way communication process, which involves people participating and sharing with each other. This is particularly important if you are targeting the 'new breed' of customers described above. The benefit of interaction is that **you're able to keep an ear to the ground to hear trends, opportunities, and feedback**. Blogs are accessible to people of all ages with varied lifestyles, enabling you to reach a number of demographics and to micro niche your small business.

People tend to perceive blog posts as honest, genuine and objective—for example, many blogs are devoted to independently reviewing or evaluating consumer products. Blogging, if done correctly, **conveys a personal message and one that is not an overt sales pitch**—consumers today are wary of marketing spiel, but a real person talking in their own voice catches their attention. Blogs typically have (and should have) an informal, conversational style, and readers can contribute by commenting on each post. Blogs can be chatty, informative, opinionated and humorous, and it's this "human" aspect of blogs that will draw people to your brand.

Messages targeted to specific groups of prospects rather than to the population as a whole, makes communication more meaningful and less intrusive and spam-like. Blogs have feedback functions so your SME can **ascertain how consumers respond to your brand**, and these are valuable opinions which will help you with future marketing strategies.

Strategically choosing your blog Titles, URL and Description are the main point of blogging for small business—they have a <u>big</u> effect on your Google rankings. Why wouldn't you want your company's webpage to be the top of the list whenever a common search term is entered into Google? How do you achieve this? By having links on your blog back to your website, ideally for the visitor to then register to get more information. And, as we discuss in the chapter on SEO, the 'anchor text' (that's the underlined text that takes the reader to your page) of the link must be key word rich.

According to Forrester Research, the largest growth in online technologies consumption (joining social networks, reading and reacting to content) comes from the 35-44 age group—an age group with influence, position, and money to spend. These managers, professionals and knowledge workers are likely to be potential clients for your small business.

In summary, an effective blog will:

- **Direct internet traffic to your main website**
- **Boost your search engine ranking**
- **Establish a web presence and build brand awareness and loyalty**
- **Generate more product sales**
- **Potentially create an additional stream of advertising income (but that's unlikely for an SME following the blogging strategy we recommend)**

> *Blogs, microblogs (a la Twitter), syndication, online communities, social networks, and widgets are changing the rules of business as we know them and will be the new must-haves for your company's success. Taken together they form the basis for an incredibly powerful toolkit that will enable you to communicate, promote your company and services, engage with, educate and listen to the customer directly, and spread your ideas and products virally so that you expand your company's reach.*
>
> **Megan Smith, Founder-CEO of Brownstone PR**

How to Set Up Your Blog

There are too many blog hosts on the internet to be able to list them all here, and they change constantly. All of our clients use **Wordpress**—a great piece of free software that can be tailored and personalised to your needs and is used by many thousands of active bloggers. Wordpress offers a variety of magazine templates so you can easily customise the layout of your blog. *lead creation* uses the following free Wordpress themes for our client blogs:

Sliding Doors

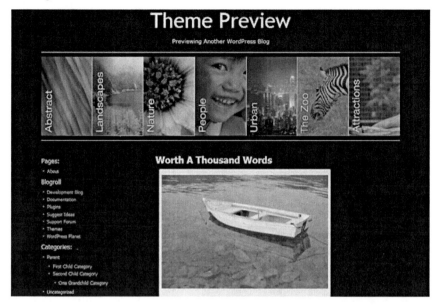

Sliding doors is an image-oriented theme on a sophisticated and professional black background, perfect for SMEs in services or professional services. The left hand column facilitates easy navigation, and the image bar at the top is interactive. This works well for business web pages with discrete categories. For example, a law firm with multiple areas of practice might have categories such as Commercial, Criminal, Family, Professional Negligence, Property, Trade Practices, and Wills and Probate.

This is the theme that I use on my blog, www.tobymarshall.com
Come and visit, join the conversation. You might have gathered that I have strong views. Tell me where you disagree. Or even, that you agree. That's always nice!

Arras

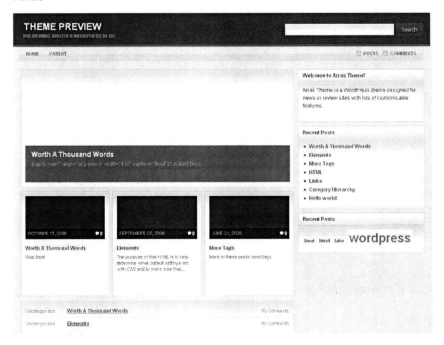

The Arras theme is easy to establish and update, and strongly resembles a news or review-oriented webpage. The layout is aesthetically pleasing, with a navigation column on the right hand side of the page, and the latest blog post sitting atop the last three posts. Both the search bar and biography box are prominent in the top right hand corner of the page.

This is the theme that my colleague Lincoln Smith uses on his blog, www.smallbusinessleads.com.au

Choose a professional-sounding URL for your blog which must include a **high traffic keyword or two** (to increase your blog's searchability). The only obstacle you might come across is finding a blog name and URL which hasn't already been taken—but this can be easily circumvented with the use of hyphens or linking words. If your company already has a creative name, take advantage of it. Examples of keyword rich URLs are ones with two or more keywords in them. Look at the name of Lincoln's blog, for example, www.smallbusinessleads.com.au and Toby' LinkedIn URL is www.linkedin.com/in/leadgenerationforsmallbusiness - not my name like 99% are: This is valuable SEO 'real estate', use it.

How to Market Through Your Blog

"Brands are about trust, and authenticity is the foundation of trust. Blogs should be written as if close friends were sharing observations over a beer." Nick Wreden, brand expert. In other words, you want customers to hear, "My small business cares about your problem and I'm giving you a solution to it, (or more information that will help you solve it)", rather than "hand over your money for this latest gadget or gizmo". But of course you **must** first make your blog findable amongst the millions of blogs already out there, for being 'findable' is the foundation of internet marketing for any small business.

So How Can You Make Your Blog Stand Out?

1. **Keywords** and Search Engine Optimisation (in Australia, it is really just Google Optimization, as Google dominates) will increase traffic to your blog, resulting in increased traffic to your main website. This will give you a greater web presence, increased brand awareness, and eventually, REVENUE. I'm on a mission to promote GO, not SEO!

2. Tags are keywords used to classify and categorise internet content. Good tagging will ensure people who are looking for you can find you. Use both general and specific keywords as tags—remember the goal is to capture as many people who are searching for anything related to your company as possible. Often, searchers misspell their search terms, so include a few commonly misspelled versions of your keywords as tags. (Think of them as the blog term for keywords)

3. Remember: **online communities are about cooperation and sharing**. If you link to other blogs, they will link to you—the more links to your blog, the higher search engine value it has. Use your blog to generate discussion about your company's product—it's the perfect way to gather feedback. Consider installing a counter on your blog to keep track of how many readers have seen your post—this will encourage more readers out of curiosity, or perhaps a lemming mentality. However, don't do it until you have optimized or you'll fall victim to the 'who wants to eat in an empty restaurant' syndrome! Install functions into your blog so readers can rate, vote on or comment on what you've written.

4. **LINK, LINK, LINK** to your business' homepage with teaser articles, stories, photos or videos. Remember, your blog is a **channel** through which to direct internet traffic to your main website. Using your blog and a combination of social bookmarking sites (explained towards the end of this chapter,) to link back to your company website, will optimize search engine results in your favor, taking you closer to the magic 'I'm Feeling Lucky' position on Google.

5. '**Pinging**' refers to notifying a server that your blog has been updated, so search engines can be updated accordingly. The site www.pingomatic.com has easy-to-follow prompts which largely automates the pinging process. Link your blog to a variety of **social bookmarking** sites, which organise, classify and categorise internet content according to keywords (called 'tags'), making links easier to share within networks and throughout the World Wide Web. Popular social bookmarking websites such as www.delicious.com, are used to search for information. The main benefit of social bookmarking is getting **free traffic from the search engines**. With social bookmarking, you can easily rank for **long tail keywords** in the search engines. Even the tiniest SME!

6. Post personal opinions (but be careful to not be so contentious as to alienate your audience) so readers can connect with a person, not a company. Above all, don't confine posts to promotional or sales material—that's just all about you. Who cares? However, your posts can and should be quite businesslike and informative. **The human side to blogging must be preserved** for readers to be engaged.

Strategies for Increasing Backlinks to Your Blog and Website

- Provide **free tools or services**. For example, if you're a Search Engine Optimization specialist, provide a link-tracking tool. If you're in web design, provide templates and plug-ins. This is called *link baiting*, and it only works if the content you are offering is unique and useful.

- **'Organic traffic'** is web traffic generated by search engines, and as you know in Australia the only one that matters is Google. To increase traffic, use search engine optimization techniques such as a sitemap, inward links, or keywords in your headings. Updating your blog regularly attracts search engine bots (known as 'spiders') to your site more regularly.

- **Social bookmarking** (explained later in this chapter in detail) through sites such as Digg, Technorati and Delicious, will also generate links back to your webpage. Viral marketing (also known as 'word of mouth') occurs when readers recommend the services of your small business to their friends and family by way of sending them a link to your blog or site. Make sure you have options such as "email to friends", "share on Facebook" or "Digg it" readily available to capitalise on this option.

Blog Design—Keep Them Coming Back For More

- Avoid clashing colors—they are tacky and unprofessional. Opt for a sophisticated and subtle color scheme which incorporates black and white plus one or two complementary colors.
- Avoid font which is too large, too small or too flowery to read.
- Avoid intrusive advertisements (banner ads or pop-ups)— just don't have them! They will damage your process of building engagement.
- Images need labels (alt tags) to help people find you in search engine listings. People often use the image search options offered by Google and other search engines, and naming your images with optimization in mind can boost your traffic.
- Make navigation simple. Most blogs already have optimized site architecture, with a clear navigation, where every page is set up to link back to the other main pages.

Blogging and Google Optimization

LINKS

- Create relevant links: You can link related posts (your own, or other bloggers), with a message below each blog reading: 'if you enjoyed this post, here are a few more you may like'. Wordpress can do this automatically, based on keywords.
- Make the links open in a new window, as opposed to opening the link so it replaces your blog. (Add target="_blank" to your link tag.) This way, your page remains open and in order to leave, your readers must close your page manually.

KEYWORDS

- Don't target a general, high-traffic keyword; you will have no chance of ranking well unless you spend many thousands of dollars. Consider using keywords that get a moderate level of more targeted traffic, resulting in more subscribers and sales. In internet marketing these are known as "the money keywords". They may not get you the most traffic, but they often bring the most profit. Lucrative keywords result in a higher ratio of buyers to visitors and are typically 'long tail keywords— a fancy term for multi word keywords. For example, some of our keywords are: 'How to advertise small business', 'small business internet marketing', 'professional services marketing online'. Though they are long, they work because if someone types this into Google, they are likely to be seriously looking for the service we provide.

- Your blog can be set up to repeat the keywords that you want to target just enough times to establish a theme. You can take full advantage of this in your post titles, your category names, the page URL names, Technorati tags, text of your permanent links that appear after each post, etc.

- The objective of all of this is to optimize your pages for search engines to find them. But be careful: don't overload your posts with too many keywords or irrelevant keywords. This is spamming and could result in your blog being removed from search engines entirely (to preserve the integrity of search engine results). More importantly, it will turn off your prospects. Remember the point? To advertise your small business for **Lead generation!**

- The title of your blog should 1) grab the reader's attention and 2) work in search queries as well—the title is your most important 'Google real estate'. Integral to your internet marketing.

FREQUENCY

- The more you post, the more you feed the search engine spider. The spider will then visit your page multiple times, by adding you to a more frequent schedule of returns. This means your pages will get indexed more often and new pages will show up faster.

- Frequently updating your blog with useful content is the first step to building your blog's audience. The content you write is what will keep readers coming back for more. Post frequently to increase the number of chances you have for your blog's content to be noticed by search engines such as Google or Technorati.

- You don't have to slave over long blog posts to get these results. Some blog software like Wordpress lets you set up your posts in advance, so that you can create a backlist of posts and have them show up regularly.

- Search engines favor blogs that are focused, tend to stay on topic, and are updated at least three times a week. The freshness of content is of paramount importance.

- Once you've established a frequent pattern of posting and you have the Googlebot coming to your site every few days, you can then link to other sites that you want crawled. These links may be in the body of each blog post, or they could be a permanent fixture, for example, on the left hand side of the page.

QUALITY

- People should find your posts useful, informative, or entertaining (ideally, all three). Make them want to return to your website in search of more content, or even subscribe.

- Watch other blogs in your niche to pick up on trends—other bloggers, especially competitors, are a valuable source of information.

- Consider 'going the extra mile' by giving away freebies such as subscriber-only content.

SUBMISSIONS

Submit Your Blog to Search Engines and Social Bookmarking Sites

- Most search engines provide a 'Submit' link (or something similar) to notify the search engine of your new blog, so those search engines will crawl it and include your pages in their results.

- Submitting your best posts to **social bookmarking** sites such Digg, Delicious and Technorati can also quickly boost traffic to your blog. Of course it's better that others do it, but you can do a few.

INTERACTIVITY

- Respond to reader comments on your blog to show you value their opinions. Start conversations—this will increase reader loyalty.

- Leave comments on other related blogs to drive new traffic. Leave your blog's URL in your comment, so you create a link back to your own blog. If someone reads a particularly interesting comment, they are likely to click on the link to visit the commentator's website.

Why use LinkedIn?

In publishing your 'Niche Newspaper', you decide the media you will use to distribute it. If your business only has time for one 'distribution channel' (one Social Network) ...

It _must_ be LinkedIn.

It's the clear cut choice if your Finance Director (you!) only has the budget of time and money to do one and you work in:

- Any small services business that sells to high end professionals or managers
- Any professional services business, small or giant, from the following list (which is the client list for our business, _lead creation_):

Financial Planners

Accountants

Lawyers

Engineering Consultants

Stock Brokers

Project Managers

Strategic Consultants

HR Consultants

Non-executive Directors (seeking more Boards)

Recruitment Firms

Business Coaches

Executive Coaches

Life Coaches

© www.leadcreation.com.au

Training Companies

Architects

Quantity Surveyors

Marketing and Branding Consultants

IT Companies

IT Support

Why is LinkedIn Essential?

It starts with there being more than 50 million professionals and knowledge workers on the site—a milestone they reached in early October 2009. Once you know your niche, you can connect with anyone in this network if you offer value and follow the networking strategies outlined in this chapter.

What can you do with LinkedIn? Well, no surprises given the title of this book—it's a powerful tool in the arsenal of small business internet marketing. A powerful tool for micro and small businesses. One that can turbo-charge the stream of prospects filling your marketing funnel (can you turbo-charge a funnel? Don't know, but it sounded good!)

Secondly, you can solve problems and issues by asking questions. There are experts on LinkedIn in almost any obscure field you can imagine. Some of these, in fact often lots of them, just love to answer questions to help people and demonstrate their knowledge.

In fact, most of them are following the golden rules of marketing outlined in this book:

- Give unconditionally
- Demonstrate expertise
- Establish a relationship
- and finally, bank the money! (OK, that's a joke. Sort of.)

What is LinkedIn?

LinkedIn is a social networking site where users integrate their business and professional contacts into an online network. Some have (stupidly) criticised it for not being open enough and for charging for too many of its services. However, after Facebook it is the most popular online social network for business professionals and managers aged 25 and over. More importantly, it makes money and so is likely to survive and grow— it's risky to invest your time and effort into a site that isn't.

Your big opportunity? Very few SMEs and small businesses are using it effectively, leaving the field wide open for professionals who have a clear strategy to get more business. There is a lot of 'low hanging fruit' waiting to be picked for at least the next 2 years. This chapter gives you clear and effective strategies, and will enable you to research, solve business problems and generate more qualified leads. And remember, that's the whole point of this book: lead generation for small businesses.

LinkedIn is a social networking website specifically aimed at creating connections between business professionals. LinkedIn passed 50 million registered users in October 2009 and is growing steadily. Its main functions are to strengthen and establish new relationships with business professionals, hence the slogan "Where Relationships Matter". On LinkedIn, you can connect with professional colleagues, meet new people, find recommended services and new contacts in your current network, allowing you to reach 50 million professionals and many of the world's major corporations.

You are at the centre of your own network, and LinkedIn creates opportunities for you to meet people who are two degrees (people who know people you know), or even three degrees away from you. The implications this has for your small business is that it could be used as a form of viral marketing which will increase brand awareness. And not through blatant advertising, but as a more credible source in positioning yourself and your company to the outside world.

More Reasons to Incorporate LinkedIn into Your Marketing Strategy

- **It's free!** LinkedIn is free to use, but companies have the option to pay to increase the features they have access to.
- **Increase your business' visibility.** By networking through LinkedIn, you will reach more potential clients than you can imagine. Also, there are options to set your profile to be indexed by Google and the other search engines which further increases your company's visibility to the big world out there.
- **LinkedIn helps you meet the right people.** LinkedIn will assist your business not only by helping you meet new clients, but also people in the same industry who are on the lookout for opportunities to deal with you.
- **Testing the waters.** Just like other people can see your company's profile, you can also see other companies' profiles. LinkedIn allows you to check out competitors' teams, clients, references and other information that's not usually available to you.

Getting More from LinkedIn

There are many different social networks around and the common questions raised are, "what is the difference?" and "which social network should I use?" While Facebook is currently the largest active online social network, LinkedIn is the **only** choice for businesses, particularly those in professional services. It's easier and way more valuable to incorporate LinkedIn into your business marketing strategy than using other social networks. And it's more likely to survive in the long term.

So where do you start? **Your profile** on LinkedIn is one of the most important brand assets you have online. It is essential that you work to keep it informative and optimized for search engines. Make sure that the URL to your company's LinkedIn profile is branded and make good use of the space you have to communicate information about your small business to viewers, but be careful not to clutter your page with too much information. Your headline shows up wherever you appear in LinkedIn (just below your name), so make sure it is as informative and clear as can be with the 120 characters you have to do it—for SEO and impact reasons, it is best to use as many of the characters as you can. For example, Toby Marshall's uses 120 characters as follows:

Small Business Internet Marketing; implementing innovative & effective lead generation, espec. for professional services

It's outcome focused and also uses our three main keywords. This makes it much more likely that searchers will find this profile—people tend to use the same terms whether searching in Google or elsewhere.

Finally, make sure that your company's website (and blog if you have one) is displayed on the company profile page.

- **Recommendations!** The point of a social network is not just to make new connections, but also to nurture existing relationships. An extremely useful feature of LinkedIn is the ability to write recommendations (testimonials) for other people (which act as a reference for other people looking to connect with them). What does this mean for you? If you give someone a good recommendation, chances are they will return the favour and write you one too.

Recommendations give your potential clients a fair idea of who you are and what to expect from you and your company. Be honest when writing recommendations and <u>only</u> write for people who you actually want to recommend. Writing recommendations just to receive one in return defeats the purpose of the system and will backfire on you. When? Well, once someone's looking for a supplier they may be looking in depth at 2 or 3 profiles. Clearly fake testimonials will put egg all over your face. Worthy of an Online Darwin Award!

One of the great but unsung benefits of LinkedIn is it makes it so much easier for people to write you a testimonial. It is easier than writing a letter, and of course has much more impact as it is broadcast so broadly. Are testimonials important for getting new clients? Absolutely, they are the single most important piece of your online <u>and</u> offline marketing—see the testimonials chapter for why, and how to get ones that work. You can also view our testimonials for *lead creation* at:

http://www.leadcreation.com.au/testimonials

- **Joining and/or leading groups** is one of the keys to improving lead generation with LinkedIn. Being part of groups that are relevant to your small business not only lets you meet new people belonging to the same group, but also opens up the opportunity for you to take part in group discussions. Creating groups is another good way of displaying your expertise in a niche. By being the leader you gain added influence within your network and people interested in your niche group will join and learn more about you.

- Be careful not to create groups that are too similar or identical to ones that already exist because they will be seen by others to be pointless or even as a desperate attempt by you or your company to grab attention (spam).

- **The strategy for starting a group?** Join 3 or 4 groups in a similar field and monitor the discussions. Look for what topics seem to interest people. Engage with a few of the active people by responding to their comments, and perhaps ask them what they think of your group idea. Then, start the group slowly by inviting people to join and by leading off some discussions. As always, don't sell, give and help while building your credibility and perception of expertise.

- **Answer (and ask) Questions!** The Question and Answer feature on LinkedIn gives a small business the perfect opportunity to position themselves as the experts in the field, just like the discussion boards. The more questions you answer, the more people will become aware of your company. Answer questions thoroughly and thoughtfully to show that you care and are willing to help. And don't blatantly sell. In fact, don't sell at all!

- Your answers can be rated by readers so make sure you don't answer questions if you don't really know what you're talking about. Gaining 'good' or 'best' answer ratings for your answers will definitely give you some added exposure.

- Asking questions will also help you gain some recognition if they promote interesting and insightful discussion. Be careful not to ask questions that go against your main objective to become positioned as the expert.

- **To get started:** Ask one or two friends to post a real question, in your core area of expertise, and then answer it really well. Then ask them to award it Best Answer—having this award then features next to all your answers in future and people are more likely to take notice of your answers. Warning: don't do more than two of these. This is a real community, don't spam it.

Creating Leads with LinkedIn

LinkedIn is one of the best social networks for a small business to implement their online marketing strategy. **Lead generation is the biggest goal that we are focusing on for our clients**. In doing so, we need to ensure that the audience we attract for our clients lead to quality leads because we are targeting the right people. There are a few steps to follow:

- When choosing the group to target, pay attention to the level of activity and not just the population of the group. It is better to be part of **a smaller group that encourages interaction** between its members than a large one with minimal activity.

    You will need to join a group in order to see its activity. Once you have joined and assessed the groups that are relevant to your company and field, narrow down your scope by disregarding the ones that don't have much discussion. The aim of this is to reduce the amount of effort wasted in trying to grab the attention of an audience who aren't listening and maximize chances of sales lead generation by communicating with people who respond.

    A large number of LinkedIn users are those who seek employment, which is expected of what is also a giant career networking website. When trying to create leads, you need to filter out the job seekers by **targeting groups that are actively**

discussing business concerns rather than employment opportunities.

- LinkedIn provides a medium by which you can share new material within a community, such as white papers or webinars. When sharing this material, try to do it within the context of a discussion as opposed to promoting a product. For example, you can start a conversation within a group by asking for feedback about an updated version of the whitepaper you've been working on.

  This is beneficial as people are given the freedom to express their views of your work and it draws your attention to any areas you can improve on. Another method to subtlety promote your work is by monitoring other conversations and responding if the **opportunity to show your expertise** arises; you may then **post a link to your whitepaper or webinar** as part of your offer to assist people.

- When joining groups for lead generation, it is a good idea to **join under an individual name as opposed to using your company's identity**. By joining a group as an individual it helps to establish a personal presence within the industry, and people you potentially want to network with will not get the impression that you are trying to sell a product (and so avoid you).

- LinkedIn is a <u>social</u> networking website, so in order to fully take advantage of this and leverage it in your small business you need to be **active in discussions** to position yourself as the expert and also receive feedback from others. Answering questions in discussions will show potential clients that you are the person and company to go to when their need for your services arise.

- The transition from LinkedIn to a company landing page can be quite abrupt. A smoother transition in the form of a **landing page designed purely for the LinkedIn visitors** could assist in creating continuity. There is no need to create a completely different page to the standard landing page you use normally, but merely to modify some text to address and welcome the users arriving from LinkedIn.

How Do You Use It?—
Try Out the Top 5 LinkedIn Tools

1. LinkedInABox

LinkedInABox displays various profile information on your blog or site in an easy to manage way. Take this as a step ahead of LinkedIn's default site-buttons that only link to your profile page. The information at LinkedInABox is displayed inside the box without having to leave the web page you are on. Information that you can choose to display are your profile summary, specialties, education, experience, public profile, recommendations, connections You can choose from six colour themes for the box or choose to put a background picture.

2. Email Linkify

If you use Firefox, Email Linkify is a script that you can use on your browser (unfortunately this script is incompatible with Internet Explorer or Google Chrome). It changes all the emails in your online inbox or websites into web links. Clicking these links will add the emails into your LinkedIn Contact List

© www.leadcreation.com.au

3. Contacts Management

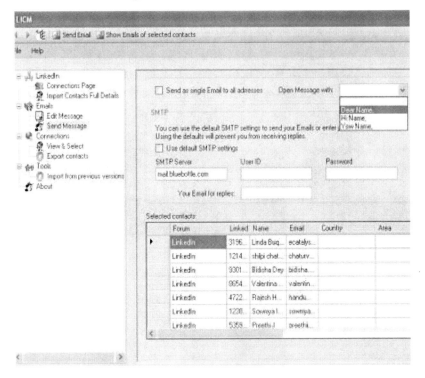

LinkedIn Contacts Management is a desktop application that functions as a mailing list manager allowing you to send emails to all your LinkedIn contacts in one go. The tool imports your LinkedIn contact list information complete with name, email, country, company, etc. You can filter this list later according to your requirements. You can also export your data in a CSV or text format.

4. LinkedIn Toolbars

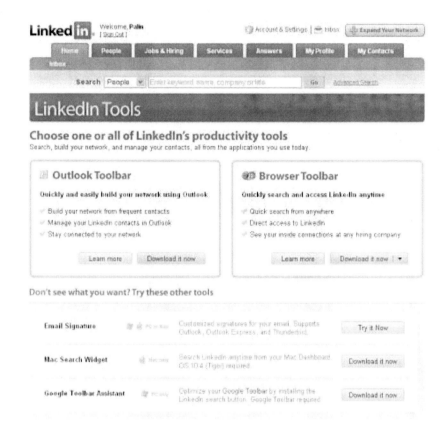

LinkedIn Tools is a set of official tools from LinkedIn itself consisting of an outlook toolbar, browser toolbar for Firefox and Internet Explorer (Internet Explorer reviews), email signature, Mac search widget, and a Google (Google reviews) toolbar assistant. With the Outlook toolbar, you can update your Outlook contacts with LinkedIn profile and receive notification when your contacts make any changes in their profiles. The browser toolbar has a search form and provides access to various LinkedIn profiles. The Jobs Insider tool in the browser toolbar allows you to check out job openings at popular job sites and connect you to people in your network who work in a recruitment company.

5. Export LinkedIn Connections

Export LinkedIn Connections—this is a tool that allows you to export your LinkedIn contacts to Microsoft Outlook, Outlook Express, Yahoo! Address Book, or Mac OS Address Book as a CSV or VCF file. Detailed instructions for each of the services are provided by LinkedIn.

Twitter in a Nutshell

Twitter is a social networking and micro-blogging service that enables you to send and read updates (known as 'tweets'). It's like blogging on a small scale, and so is sometimes called microblogging. Each post is 140 characters in length, so you need to be able to express yourself succinctly, to capture attention.

Twitter users 'follow' each other, that is, choose to receive the tweets of another user in a real-time feed. For business? It's a communications platform that helps businesses quickly share information and build relationships with interested parties and potential customers/clients, and gather real-time market intelligence and feedback. It's used as:

- An information tool allowing you to provide information to others
- A communication tool. You can respond to other peoples' tweets, and vice versa. It facilitates dialogue and conversation.

Will Twitter survive and prosper? Don't know, my crystal ball smashed last week. A question we can answer is: Are there real online marketing advantages for small businesses now? The answer to that is Yes!

However, the _real_ reason we put our clients onto Twitter? Every Tweet creates a unique web page, and if every tweet has a link back to your website, Google will rank you more highly starting in about December 2009. So, the point is getting higher rankings and then more customers on Google. Not about following Obama or Kevin07 and learning how they passed their day!

So if the prime reason is to optimize the website of your small business, then keep your Tweets simple. Most importantly keep them to a theme so you don't need to constantly dream up new ideas. Ideally this then will display your expertise, and ideally have a personal, even a humorous, touch. Dreaming up or digging out themes for our clients is a lot of fun! For example, see Toby's Online Darwins—awards for people who are so stupid online that they Deserve to Die! (Have you read the Darwin Awards books or seen the movie? Great black comedy.)

Follow him at *http://twitter.com/Toby_Marshall*

From 'Twitter 101'

(http://business.twitter.com/twitter101/resources)

Twittering is the sound birds make when they communicate with each other—an apt description of the conversations here. As it turns out, because Twitter provides people with real-time public information, it also helps groups of people mimic the effortless way a flock of birds move in unison.

When Twitter users log on, they see a feed of the most recent tweets— the more frequently you 'tweet' the more likely followers are to see your profile. Post links to your blog, your webpage, or any other interesting and relevant articles, along with a comment to make people want to click through. To view the conversations happening in real time about your product, brand, or company, use search.twitter.com—you can do this with or without setting up a profile first.

Harnessing social networking enables your small business to take advantage of how media consumption is changing – and use it to establish and enhance relationships with customers.

Using Twitter is as Easy as 1, 2, 3!

1. **Updates** are best used to reach all your followers who are monitoring Twitter at that moment — consistent with a list building strategy rather than an online social networking strategy

2. **Replies** are updates that begin with @username, public messages addressed to a particular member. Members don't need to be following you to receive a reply, but if they're not following you, they can safely choose to ignore you without appearing rude. If you're having a long conversation, which others might find annoying, avoid using replies — use direct messages instead. Annoy people, and they will stop following you. Use replies specifically when you want everybody or a group of people included in your discussion

3. **Direct messages** referred to as DM's are private, and they're the closest you can get to e-mail communication using Twitter. Use direct messages when it's inappropriate to reach the community-at-large. Direct messages are rarely ignored, and they're essential to cultivating real relationships using Twitter

Why Twitter is Fast Emerging as an Important New Marketing Medium

1. **SPEED and CONVENIENCE**. Can you spare three minutes of your busy working day? Perhaps you have a moment during your commute, or while you're waiting for a meeting to begin. It only takes 140 characters—if you're lucky, you can fit in two whole sentences! These messages are quick to write, easy to read, public, controlled by the recipient and exchangeable anywhere. The end result? A powerful, real-time communications medium

2. **EASE**. Twitter is simple to use—if Granny can type, she can tweet

© www.leadcreation.com.au

3. **DISTRIBUTION**. As of February 2009, Twitter had 7 million users, and was the fastest-growing social network, growing by 1382%, as compared to the popular Facebook, which grew by 228%. The Global Index Chart, published by Nielsen, states that the average time spent on a website is 51 seconds. The average time spent on Twitter is 9.1 minutes. As of July 2009, according to Alexa, the Web Information Company, Twitter is ranked 25th in terms of generating web traffic in the US, and 13th in Australia

- Twitter is the fastest-growing, hottest social media property at the time of writing this, with the potential to be bigger than Facebook and MySpace—and it can even compete with Yahoo and Google for news
- Twitter reveals the human side to your company, giving it personality
- Twitter provides useful information people won't get anywhere else as quickly, acting as a platform for announcing news and events
- Twitter allows you to respond to comments, requests, feedback and complaints in REAL TIME

Twitter gives you the chance to communicate with customers on their terms, creating friendly relationships. Customers may have minor **complaints** or **suggestions** for improvement that they would never bother to contact you about. You can then incorporate this invaluable **customer feedback** into your future plans. By analysing what customers are saying about your small business brand you can effectively use Twitter to gather interesting information from the market in real-time. If you discover a complaint on Twitter it will be possible for you to **provide solutions** to your customers in a timely way. Listening and engaging on social networks leads to happier customers, passionate advocates, a better online reputation, and increased brand awareness. It can also make a stuffy ad business look a bit more modern in 2010!

Start Tweeting!

Social networking is no longer just for tech-savvy teens. Setting up a Twitter account is as easy – just log on to twitter.com and follow the prompts. Make it stand out with an attention-grabbing profile picture, colour scheme and design. Perhaps a headshot of you as the default picture, and the company logo as the background. Because your bio can only be 160 characters, you may want to design your own background which includes more information about yourself and your brand.

What will you Tweet about?

Well, that depends on your Twitter goals, which may be building deeper relationships, collecting feedback, increasing your online presence, making sales or providing customer service.

1. **Your business**, e.g.: "just got home—phew, that case took some work, but it was so rewarding". OR "almost cried when our client got the compensation she deserved. Justice prevails!"
2. **Your products**, e.g.: "working on a new eBook! Will keep you updated on its progress!" (But not too many like this as it's all about you.)
3. **Your blog**, e.g.: "hate spam so much I wrote an entire blog entry about it → [insert link]". OR "just blogged the key to prospering in the economic recovery! Check it out at [insert link]. Too long to Tweet!"
4. **Interesting and relevant content.** Give people a reason to follow you by being interesting and challenging. Constant product links or event announcements will lead to people 'unfollowing' you, thinking you're a spammer – and they'd be right. Link occasionally to interesting but related articles, so

potential customers see your small business as an asset to their Twitterstream.

Strategies for using Twitter as a Marketing Tool

BE DIRECT. We've all heard that users of social networks such as Twitter have learned to multitask to the point of developing mild ADD. Tweets are short, and need to be attention grabbing and direct. Avoid cryptic posts unless they are engaging enough for readers to follow up on. Tweet strategically. As marketers say, using social media shrinks the emotional distance between your company and your present and potential customers. Being confined to 140 characters means no waffle. Get straight to the point. If you are posting links (say, links to your blog, your LinkedIn account, or your company webpage) you must **use a URL shortening tool**—some links are longer than 140 characters themselves, leaving no room for a tantalising comment. Try www.TinyURL.com or www.bit.ly, which are both really simple and effective to use. Sometimes Twitter will automatically shorten a URL for you.

BE ENGAGING. *Follow other users and they will follow you.* Remember— online communities and social networks are about sharing, interacting and contributing. Following users who are also potential customers can give your small business an idea of market niches you could focus on, or customer needs yet to be met.

On Twitter, people can view your updates by searching for specific keywords or by following your account. This means that if you are compelling enough, people on Twitter will choose to view your updates by searching or following. And remember—the process of 'unfollowing' someone is even easier!

Dry and boring Tweets rarely draw many people. Successful Twitter marketers are diverse in the strategies they adopt. Some are personal and chatty, while some just include mostly automated information. But the one thing they have in common is that their messages are compelling.

Facilitate conversation by asking thoughtful questions or taking opinion polls—**get your followers to respond to you**. This not only tells consumers that their opinions are valued, but also is invaluable feedback for your small business. Start discussions: give personal opinions on links, ask people for their thoughts, stir up a little controversy. In the words of Eric Brantner (business copywriter and SEO expert), *interactivity is the key to social media success.*

Don't forget your classic marketing techniques—use humor to engage readers. Always post an engaging title or tantalising comment with your links—what are the chances of someone clicking on a random URL? Participate within the community—Twitter is a community-based social networking site. Show interest in other businesses and people and they are more likely to show interest in you and your brand.

INTERACT. Posting links with @username automatically creates a link to that person's account—alerting them to your own profile, and facilitating an interactive dialogue. Keep an eye out for @mentions of your own business, because they're often sent by present or potential clients expecting a reply.

To engage with and show respect for other Twitter users, you can repost their messages and give them credit. This is called **retweeting**, and generally looks something like this: "RT @Username: 'Original message'." Retweeting is another popular way of starting a conversation.

On the right-hand side column of your Twitter homepage is an ever-changing list of **Trending Topics**, which are the ten most mentioned and most searched-for terms on Twitter. Pay attention to these, as they will give you a clue as to what people are interested in. If a Trending Topic is relevant to your business, use it in a tweet, so your profile appears every time someone conducts a search using that term. A **hashtag** is just the # symbol followed by a term, e.g.: #accountant. This is another handy way of making your profile more searchable. Hashtags don't necessarily have to be trending topics, but with a little strategic tweeting, you can get it there. For instance, you can post "how are we going to survive this #GFC?" Your message would then be part of Twitter search results for "#GFC," and if enough people use the same hashtag at once, the term will appear in Twitter's Trending Topics.

Keep an ear to the ground for comments about your company, brand and products—and be prepared to address concerns, handle complaints, offer customer service or thank people for praise.

> A few more **interactive strategies suggested by Twitter101**:
> - Offer Twitter-exclusive coupons or deals
> - Take people behind the scenes of your company
> - Post pictures from your offices, stores, warehouses, etc.
> - Share sneak peeks of projects or events in development

DON'T SPAM. If your messages are meaningful enough, readers will 'retweet' them. Post regularly for maximum visibility—2/3 times per week is probably the maximum. If you don't have the time to maintain this, probably better to focus on just one social network like LinkedIn. Small businesses seeking marketing results online need to <u>focus</u>. Three times a week is not time-consuming. But know the difference between posting often and spamming. Avoid over-promoting your product and coming across as salesy; why would anyone follow a Twitterer who is blatantly selling something and offering no value?

Do not make promotion the sole focus of your Twitter account. Instead, post meaningful, relevant and readable content that your subscribers are going to look forward to. Post all kinds of <u>relevant</u> information about your company, your products, the industry—but look for angles to make it interesting and always look for ways to offer gifts of information or resources. Overwhelming followers with me, me, me will cause them to abandon you.

"It's not about trying to sell your product, but more building relationships with customers and potential customers," says Dave Brookes who is THE marketing department of Teusner Wines. "This is about building trust as well as relationships—and that comes from not selling."

Spamming, which may lead to your profile being deleted altogether, and leave your company's reputation in ruins, can include the following:

- Posting duplicate updates repeatedly
- Posting the same update via a number of Twitter profiles
- 'Following churn'—making people notice you by following then unfollowing them repeatedly

If you behaved like this in the offline world you would be despised and probably perceived as a moron. Why do people think it's acceptable online? Peanut brains!

KEYWORDS, KEYWORDS, KEYWORDS. Look at trends, and make your posts relevant to those trends. Study the 'trending topics' which have generated many searches. If there is one there which is relevant to your Tweet, use it! It will increase traffic to your Twitter profile. Enough hype surrounding your Tweets could make your brand or business a trending topic in itself, if you generate interest and give your followers a reason to retweet your tweets.

Consider the following case study: Source: Kenji Brian Sakamoto,
Internet Marketer

> *An excellent example of a successful social network marketing strategy was a sale run by a major retailer on a specific date, where the company offered flip flops for the price of $1/pair. The moment this news hit Twitter, it was repeated over and over, and within hours the company was a trending topic (one of the top posted-about topics on the network) and all the store's retail outlets were swamped with customers. The cost of this marketing campaign was tiny, but the number of customers tempted to the store by the promise of cheap sandals was high—and after making the trip, a good percentage of those customers most likely spent money on other products as well.*

TIME YOUR TWEETS. For optimum visibility, aim for your tweets to be at the top of the list when your followers log on. This means, don't Tweet while they're sleeping, but don't tweet during peak hour either—your message will be lost in the crowd. Monitor your Twitter feed to see if you can find a gap in the conversation during business hours to jump in. A small business has to be smart to break through the noise.

GET FOLLOWERS. Follow relevant Twitterers yourself—when you do this, that Twitterer receives a notification and can check out your own profile, building web traffic. Of course, don't blindly follow other Twitterers, select them carefully and consider whether or not they'll be interested in what you have to say. And whether in the longer term, after you've earned the right, they might be interested in the services of your small business.

Use **search.twitter.com** to search for people you know or want to target, by location, keyword, industry, interests, hashtags, or popularity.

Genuine engagement with a network of existing followers is best way to get new followers. You can automate the process using www.tweetlater.com.

Follow the example of PenguinBooksUK, a company that searches for Twitterers with the words 'books', 'reading', 'literature', etc. in their profile biographies to follow, as these are the people who are more likely to follow them back.

PenguinBooksUK is also the perfect example of a business that tweets interactively and engagingly, having recently run several well-received games, for example, for followers to summarise their favorite book in 140 characters (competition #shortpenguin), or to guess which novel a character comes from (competition #fictionalpeople). Their tweet:

> *Does anyone fancy another game of #shortpenguin, where you summarise a book in 140 characters? Will retweet the smartest/funniest/weirdest.*
>
> **- 3:04 AM Jul 8th from web**

When you follow somebody, they'll generally get an email notification from Twitter. But, many people turn off those notifications to preserve inbox space, so don't assume someone knows you're on Twitter just because you've followed them.

You can measure the value of Twitter by using tools to **figure out how much traffic your websites are receiving from Twitter**. Alternatively, if you choose to offer deals via Twitter, use a unique coupon code so that you can tell how many people heard about that particular promotion through Twitter.

BE A RESOURCE. Establish yourself as an **expert or a leading authority**. Give insight into hot industry topics, link out to other resources, engage in discussions and answer questions. Focus on **quality tweets over quantity**, but if possible, aim for quantity too—this will increase your visibility, by increasing the chance of your tweets appearing near the top of your followers' news feeds. Post links to articles and sites you think your followers would find interesting—even if (or, especially if!) they're not your sites or about your small business.

BE UNIQUE. Find a unique use for your Twitter account: maybe it can be a one-on-one customer service tool? Or a forum for public opinion polls for products? Having a unique purpose for being on Twitter, instead of just shooting out all-over-the-place updates, will help you build a solid base of followers.

How to Create Your Own Twitter Account in Six Easy Steps

1. Sign-up and post a profile. Visit Twitter.com and click on the "Get Started—Join" button in the middle. You fill in your full name, preferred user name, password and e-mail address. Remember that the user name is what people will see with an "@" symbol in front of it. Brand yourself professionally. Choose a professional Twitter name using your full name or some combination of your name and your major keyword that sounds good and is easy to remember.

2. Write some updates/tweets. Post a link to a news article you liked with a one line comment, mention an interesting thought you had, but don't tell everyone what you are cooking for dinner. Just write something.

3. To find potential clients, browse around the web on your favourite blogs, people's Facebook profiles etc. When you see a Twitter box that tells you what they are doing, click on it. That will bring you to their profile and then you just click on the "Follow" button on the top left to follow them. Most times they will follow you back, meaning one more person will see your tweets. You can get started by following me: Toby Marshall on Twitter - @tobym

4. How to post URLs. Twitter is based on 140 character Tweets. If you have a really long URL, that doesn't leave much room for most people on Twitter, use www.TinyURL.com to take a long URL and make it short. Give it a shot if you have a long URL that you want to market on Twitter.

5. Monitor conversations about your company. You can monitor what people are saying about any person, company or brand just by searching for them in the engine. This is quite useful from a marketing and PR standpoint. You can subscribe to specific companies twitters by RSS to keep updated.

How to "chat". Using the @ symbol before someone's Twitter username is how people have "conversations" in Twitter. This makes their username a link to their profile so other people can follow the conversation (sort of). For example if you wrote "@tobym thanks for the cool chapter on Social Networking" that would be a way of telling me you liked this information.

The Top Ten Reasons for Using Twitter

(After the prime <u>marketing</u> reason: of getting more traffic to your site)

1. **Simplicity** - Twitter is easier for people to understand than many other social media sites. There are only a few Twitter concepts to learn: how to create a profile, follow, update, reply, search, retweet, and send direct messages

2. **Networking** - You are able to find people with the same interests as you, and as you follow them, you are able to learn about great articles and other relevant information that may be of use to you

3. **Traffic** - Twitter is a blogger's dream, you can tweet links to your blog, website etc. But remember not to make it too salesy, otherwise people will stop following you!

4. **List Building** - Twitter is a great tool to cultivate a following in the niche market of your small business

5. **Branding** - You may use Twitter to brand and market yourself to followers. Through Twitter many people are getting to know each other, who would not have had the opportunity to meet in real life. Even people who choose not to follow someone can still learn about their business. Keep this in mind: It's not what you know or who you know, but who knows, likes, trusts and respects YOU

6. **Communicating** - You can send direct messages to communicate with your potential clients

7. **Research** - Twitter is an excellent tool for researching and keeping up with world developments. You don't need to follow people, or for them to follow you, to read their tweets and click on their links

8. **Discovery** - We can learn new things on Twitter, even when we're not looking.

9. **Mobility** - Wherever you are, you are only a tweet away. As more and more people use mobile phones and text messaging, the compact 140 character format makes Twitter easy to access

10. **Fun** - Twitter is a blast! It's a giant party, and the black tie is definitely optional (OK, maybe you need to be under 40 to think that!)

Making your Tweet count

- **Think**. The first rule of Twitter is to tweet **strategically.** Since you only have 140 characters to sell yourself or an idea, you don't want to waste even one single character with fluff, dribble, or anything ineffective. Although you may choose to 'let your hair down' sometimes and tweet about something mundane or insignificant, you still need to put a certain spin on it. Whatever your objectives are on Twitter, tweet from that angle or with that goal in mind—even if you are only talking about your breakfast.

For example, if you are a strategy consultant, instead of tweeting,

"Contact me for a new strategy :-)"

As this is way too salesy and dumb, you could tweet:

"Finding the best solution is the key to prospering in this slowly recovering market"

Find your angle, and work it! It will help you to say a lot more with fewer words.

- **Share**. Contribute to the Twitterverse, and good "Twitter Karma" will come back to you! If you're a giver, you will be rewarded with more followers and you'll gain more social capital along the way. Don't overload Twitter with every single little article you come across, but if you think that it can add value to the lives of others, share it. It shows that you are a valuable resource, too.

- **Humor**. Whatever sense of humor you have, there is someone on Twitter who will appreciate it. Even if it's quirky, it's a very easy way to reveal who you really are without making yourself vulnerable or saying too much. It makes tweeting more enjoyable, and those particular individuals more memorable.

- **Interact**. Answer others' questions. When you can't think of anything to tweet, start reading others' tweets. Be helpful and maybe start a conversation with someone who you don't know so well...yet :-)

- **Create**. Break all the rules and just let your thoughts spill out. Every now and then you have to go a little crazy. When life spills out, let your tweets spill out. Need...coffee...now!!! Ever felt like that? When you feel that way, tweet that way. It lets everyone know that you are genuine, and not just someone trying to blast your own marketing messages. This creates your own online personality and makes people realise that you are a real person!

- **Stand out**. Make use of special HTML characters. Another cool trick you can use to spice up an otherwise boring tweet is to add html "dingbats" to your messages. Add stars, flowers, and even airplanes to your expressions!

Twitter is a surprisingly effective way of communicating with businesses to foster relationships for fun and profit. That's why so many people use it; it's fun, easy to use, and most of all, effective. Say more with less, and have a good time doing it!

Don't make these Three Mistakes on Twitter!
From Christopher Boyer, marketing expert.

Mistake #1: Not participating enough...
or participating too much
Creating a social media account for a business is easy to do (you can sign up for a Twitter account and begin "tweeting" within a minute!), but it's not easy to maintain. Trends show that more people are flocking to Twitter, but many people are abandoning Twitter after only using it once.

Participating in the conversation of social media is a time commitment and there is one thing a marketer doesn't have an abundance of: free time. On the flipside, social media accounts that are too active are perceived by others to be "contributing to the noise" and are thus ignored. Maintain a fine balance in updating your social media—two to three Tweets per week at minimum. For a small business, maybe ten a week minimum?

Mistake #2: Mistaking social media for
traditional marketing – it's not.
Social networking is not about broadcasting. It's best for conversations, dialogue and interaction. Mistaking social media as another broadcast vehicle will diminish its effectiveness. Businesses that make this mistake tend to set up a Twitter account then not follow anyone (but expect others to follow them!)

Mistake #3—Trying to control your brand
on social media
Another mistake that businesses face with social media marketing, is trying to control their brand. Many businesses feel that they need to shut down any non-flattering mentions of their company that appear online.

But the reality is: social media is about openness and freedom of speech. Web 2.0 provides a democratisation of content, where anyone can state their opinions; report on news in their own way; and distribute this widely (and easily) to large networks. The concept of controlling your brand is antiquated and has been replaced by the concept of managing your reputation.

Reasons People give for Not using Twitter

- Twitter takes up time
- Twitter takes you away from other productive work
- Without a strategy, it's just typing
- There are other ways to do this
- Twitter only has a few million people using it (only!)
- Twitter doesn't replace direct email marketing
- Twitter opens the company up to more criticism and griping

Reasons why you Absolutely Should

- Twitter helps organise great instant meet-ups (tweetups)
- Twitter works well as an opinion poll
- Twitter helps direct people's attention to relevant information
- Twitter at events helps people build an instant "backchannel" (can be scary for a speaker!)
- Twitter breaks news faster than other sources
- Twitter gives businesses a glimpse at what status messaging can do for an organisation.
- Twitter brings great minds together, and gives you daily opportunities to learn (if you look for it, and/or if you follow the right people)

- Twitter gives your critics a forum, allowing you to study them. At least you know what they're saying if you're there
- Twitter helps with lead generation

Useful Twitter Sites:

http://www.twitip.com/

www.mashable.com

www.tweefind.com

Social Bookmarking Explained

Social Bookmarking is a method by which web browsers can share websites and pages of interest with other internet users. It's called bookmarking because users can create accounts on websites (such as Digg, Delicious, Reddit, etc) and "tag" these websites, which are then saved privately for them. Bookmarked websites are categorized according to the tags they are assigned, so other users can search for their particular topics of interest and find all websites listed under the specific topic area. Account users can choose to share these websites publicly or privately with selected users. Many social bookmarking websites provide account holders with the feature of being able to rate pages that other users have tagged and shared. Therefore, relevant and interesting sites will be given credit and as a result will encourage more people to view the linked websites.

What are the Implications for Marketing?

Well obviously bookmarking could help website owners generate more traffic. For example, if a visitor to a website finds a particular article or blog post interesting to them, they may logon to their respective account at a social bookmarking website and tag the site, then share it with their friends or the general public. The more people who rate the link highly, the more viewers are likely to also visit that page. This provides a feedback effect which can start out with only a few visitors but end up creating a chain reaction leading a lot of users to the bookmarked webpage, who may give more positive ratings which in turn will lead more people to view it.

The popularity of social bookmarking assists companies in generating leads (through generating traffic). Social bookmarking can be leveraged in search engine optimization to boost a website's Google page ranking, and increase its visibility on search results. Logically, if a page that has not been indexed by Google is tagged on a social bookmarking website, it will generate more page views which will help a web spider pick it up and index it.

You can create direct links from your website (and blog posts) to social bookmarking sites. This provides visitors with an easy way to add the website to their personal list of favourites and share it with others. Links or buttons that are located close to blog posts and easily seen can lead to an increase in social bookmarking activity, which in turn may generate more traffic to the page.

Top 5 Social Bookmarking Sites to Use

These sites were chosen based on Google page rankings.

- o **Technorati**
- o **Delicious (formerly del.icio.us)**
- o **Digg**
- o **Reddit**
- o **Stumbleupon**

Top Social Bookmarking sites	Google rank*
1. http://technorati.com/	9/10
2. http://slashdot.org/	9/10
3. http://digg.com/	8/10
4. http://www.stumbleupon.com/	8/10
5. http://www.reddit.com/	8/10
6. http://delicious.com/	8/10
7. http://www.mixx.com/	8/10
8. http://www.propeller.com/	8/10
9. http://buzz.yahoo.com/	7/10
10. http://www.newsvine.com/	7/10
11. http://www.blinklist.com/	7/10
12. http://www.diigo.com/	7/10
13. http://www.kaboodle.com/	6/10
14. http://www.twine.com/	6/10
15. http://www.dzone.com/links/index.html	6/10
16. http://faves.com/home	6/10
17. http://www.clipmarks.com/	5/10
18. http://www.fark.com/	4/10
19. http://www.blogmarks.net/	4/10

* As of October 27th 2009.

An In-Depth Look at the Specifics of Social Bookmarking Sites

1) Technorati in a Nutshell

Technorati is a social media blogosphere, primarily an Internet search engine for searching blogs, but it also interconnects search functions for video, pictures, news, and pretty much any page that consists of a feed. The name Technorati itself, is a word that originated from two words, pointing to the technological version of literati, or intellectuals. As of June 2008, Technorati had indexed 112.8 million blogs and over 250 million pieces of tagged social media. They also use and contribute to open source software, that is an approach to the design, development and distribution of software, offering practical accessibility to a software's source code.

How does Technorati benefit my small business?

If you own a blog or website, and would like other people to find you, Technorati is an excellent resource to drive targeted traffic. First, you'll need to understand how to add your blog in Technorati and more about Technorati Tags.

How to add my blog in Technorati?

It's a very simple process; once you have created an account, just go to the Technorati Claim Your Blog page and follow the directions. To "Claim your blog" essentially means that you are proving your ownership of your blog to Technorati, to include your name, photo and description next to your blog on any Technorati search result.

What are Technorati tags?

Think of a tag as a simple category name, this is used to describe the subject matter or topic of a blog post. People can categorize their posts, photos and videos with any tag that makes sense and of course, use their major keywords (remember keywords are how people find your small business). The tag name can be anything, but it should be descriptive and not spammed with too many keywords. Only use tags that are relevant to the post. You do not need to include the brackets, just the descriptive keyword for your post.

What's the point of using Technorati tags in your blog?

Firstly, to get your blog posts onto Technorati's tag pages in an organised, structured way. That means people searching or browsing through those tag pages will be able to find your blog posts - more exposure, more traffic, therefore more readers for your blog. Also, these tag pages often get indexed on Google, and Technorati tag pages commonly appear high in Google search results lists due to the high number of blog posts pointing to these tag pages. So, if your blog is linked to from a tag page, someone searching Google is more likely to come across your posts.

Methods of adding tags

If your blog platform already supports categories and RSS/Atom (e.g. Word Press, Movable Type or Type Pad), just assign categories to your posts and publish via RSS/Atom. Technorati will then automatically use those categories from your feed for its tags (This is called the Ping Method). If you want to include tags manually on your blog, you are able to make up any tags you like, use them in your posts, and Technorati should include them on its tag pages. For More help, Go to the Technorati Tags page to get the code format that you'll need to use for your tags, or, you can check out a few of the Technorati Tools to automate the tagging process.

You can also submit additional content and references to Technorati's tag pages via Blurbs, which can be added directly to the page. Blurbs also link back to relevant sites or your Technorati profile where readers can see your blogs, other blurbs, watch lists and favourites.

Monitoring your tags: Technorati Favourites and Watch lists

What are Technorati Favourites?

Blogs are added on a daily basis and sometimes you just want to see a few of your favorite blogs that you usually follow. Therefore Technorati have created, Technorati Favourites. This feature will serve as your bookmarks within Technorati.

To use Technorati Favourites, just create an account and log in (if you haven't already). Then simply visit your <u>Favourites page</u>.

How do I add to my Favourites?

There are lots of ways to add blogs to your Favourites.

- Click the Favourites icon () from any search result or tags page. You can search for new Favourites in <u>Blog Finder</u>, a third party application tool.
- You can also <u>import URLs</u> from other tools and services.
- Use the bookmarklet. Drag this link to your browser's toolbar and click it from any blog to add to your Favourites. <u>» Add to Technorati Favourites</u>
- Favourites will accept any valid URL, but it works best for sites that update a lot, like blogs.

How do I tag my Favourites?

You can tag your Favourites with words or phrases like "lead generation"" or "internet marketing." To create tags, go to the <u>Blogs by Favourites</u> tab and click on the "edit tags" link next to the tag icon, underneath the blog title. Enter as many tags as you like; separate each tag with a space, and if you want to use more than one word as one tag, use double quotes around the phrase. Once you are finished typing all your tags, then click "Add tags." Clicking on a tag in the left-hand list will show you all the recent posts tagged with that term. To get back to your general Favourites page, click on the My Favourites link in the page title.

Watch lists

A Technorati watch list for a URL (or a search word or phrase,) is an automatic periodic search on Technorati for that URL or search term, where the live updated search results are brought to you via an RSS feed, so that you don't have to keep going back to Technorati to repeat the search.

The standard way to create a watch list is to search on Technorati for a particular URL, word or phrase; then, in the search results list, it'll give you an option via a "Make this a Watch link" to create a watch list for that URL or search term. If you click that link, Technorati takes you to its "Add a Watch list" page with your search term displayed in a box. Check it's correct and then click the 'add' button. It cleverly creates a unique RSS feed for that search and displays the URL for that feed. Just copy the feed URL given and paste it into your feed reader in the usual way.

Summary:

Sign up for a Technorati account.

- Once you sign up, you'll be asked if you have a blog to claim. Go ahead and complete this process.
- Now that you have completed the previous process, you can start tagging your posts. If you've claimed your blog successfully, it should automatically update to Technorati.
- Make sure you regularly generate new content and monitor that content using favourites and watch lists.

How to Use Technorati

- **Step 1**: Sign up for a free Technorati membership. You need to supply a valid email address, preferred user name and password. You will then be instructed to choose topics that interest you, so that the Technorati system can recommend good reading material for you.

- **Step 2**: Once you are enrolled, go to your Favourites, located near the top of the Technorati website when you are logged in.

- **Step 3**: Once inside your Favourites, notice the two fields to the left allowing you to enter a URL and some descriptive tags for any web page. This feature will serve as your bookmarks within Technorati. Enter a valid URL of any web page, and then enter some tags. For example, if the website is about women's health, enter "women's, health, fitness" or something similar. This will allow you to search your bookmarks later.

- **Step 4**: To view your bookmarked Favourites within Technorati at any time, simply click on Favourites near the top of the Technorati website when you are logged in. You can choose to view "Posts from Favourites" or "Favorite Blogs". The former will allow you to view individual blog entries within the bookmarked website if it is a blog. The latter is just a list of the websites you enjoy reading.

2) Mmm...Delicious!

What is Delicious?

A social bookmarking website which allows users to bookmark websites they find interesting and think other people will find interesting too.

- The bookmarked links are organised according to tags, which are keywords of the general topics and areas the link pertains to.
- The links are also ranked according to how many other people have bookmarked them. Highly-ranked links are more visible and thus generate a lot of web traffic.

Get on the front page!

The front page of Delicious shows the most popular links according to numbers of bookmarks. The Delicious front page has the potential to directly send about 1,000 – 3,000 visitors to a page in one day. As well as the initial surge of traffic that comes from being on the front page of Delicious, bookmarks draw repeat traffic over time as users return to the links that they have bookmarked.

Getting on the Delicious homepage means you'll get web traffic not only from Delicious itself, but from the content aggregator **popurls.com**. Popurls.com is a collection of the most popular links on Delicious, Digg, Reddit, and several other social bookmarking sites. Popurls.com by itself will generate a few hundred more visitors.

The front page of Delicious shows the twelve most popular (i.e. most bookmarked) pages. If a page from your website makes it to the front page and can stay there for a few hours, it will receive about a thousand visitors, generate even more bookmarks, and gain exposure. More bookmarks = more repeat traffic.

Repeat traffic: the biggest strength of Delicious (and other social bookmarking sites) compared to social networking. Social networking sites can create a quick rush of traffic, but it might not last. With Delicious, you will always receive a flow of repeat traffic as users return to the pages they have bookmarked.

Why be Popular on Delicious?

1. It generates traffic, links and increases your overall exposure
2. It builds name recognition/brand awareness and a reputation as an authority in your field

These two outcomes form a virtuous cycle - more traffic leads to a better reputation, and vice versa.

What Kind of Content gets on the Front Page?

1 – Resource Lists

Just about everybody could do with the convenience of getting all the sources and materials they need on any given subject from one page only. Creating a resource list doesn't require a lot of knowledge or experience – though it may take some time to do your research. This can be delegated to a junior staff member.

A collection of resources on a single webpage is the ultimate linkbait. They do not require much thought, or even great copywriting, to create. Resource lists are timeless and their informational value is less likely to decline with changes in current events.

> **For your resource list to be bookmarked it must contain an overwhelming collection of information which cannot possibly be digested in one sitting.**

2 – Guides and Tutorials

Step-by-step and do-it-yourself guides regularly get bookmarked by users who think "this is going to be useful later on".

Marketing Effectively With Delicious

1. You'll have to network

Add people to your network, view their links, and share your links with them. It will greatly increase your click-through rate if other Delicious users perceive your profile as trustworthy and credible.

Brainstorm ideas that will:

1) Utilise popular keywords and phrases

2) Be relevant to your business' SEO strategy

The result? A boost in your search engine rankings

Include a link to your Delicious page from your website and blog so others can add you. Request that your existing blog commenters, LinkedIn contacts, email contacts and Twitter followers add you.

2. Have a specific purpose/create focused content

Pages that become popular on Delicious receive inbound links. Pages with inbound links rank well with search engines. As well as making your content intrinsically interesting and linkable, use keywords and phrases to appease the search engines.

Choose the title of your links properly (for every link you post in Delicious, you need to supply four things: the Title, the URL, a description - e.g. why you found this site important enough to bookmark, any critique you may have of it etc, and tags). What to title your links takes a little consideration as you want it to complement your existing SEO strategy. Not only will well-formulated title and description text take your links to the top of the search results page, it will also generate a higher click through rate.

3. Brand yourself

If you can make it to the front page repeatedly, people will remember you and start to view you as an expert or authority on your subject. Therefore, it's effective to keep your Delicious content focused on one primary topic, directly or indirectly related to your business. Use your name, company name, or combination of the two, as your Delicious profile name to make it easier for users to recognise you.

Summary so far

- Pages on the front page of Delicious receive a few thousand visitors
- It is basically a place to store all of your favorite pages
- Accurately titling, describing and tagging your bookmarks is key

How to get People to Bookmark Your Page, *and* make the Front Page

- Strong, attention-grabbing titles are important. A strong title will increase the amount of click-throughs.
- Create something that people will want to use in the future—not something temporarily or transiently interesting.

Cater to the masses

Don't waste your time trying to get something to the front page that doesn't fit with the interests of Delicious users. Study what types of content are popular and find ways to merge these with your business.

Get your article in front of as many people as possible so they will consider bookmarking it. There are two main ways of doing this:
- **Social voting websites:** e.g. Digg or Reddit: if your article is a success

in these social voting websites, you'll gain bookmarks and new readers. Your goal is to get your blog to be viewed as much as possible. Voting websites are the fastest way to accomplish this.

- **Targeted email pitches:** Sending emails to websites in your niche is also a useful way to pick up traffic. A link from a popular, relevant website with a large readership ensures that your article is exposed to many readers and increases its likelihood of being bookmarked.

Show the number of bookmarks on the page—use the Tagometer Badge

Delicious will provide you with the HTML code for a Tagometer Badge, to insert on to your website or blog. This badge serves two functions:

- Makes it easier for visitors to bookmark the page
- Shows how many people have already bookmarked (remember the lemming mentality—users like to bookmark links which are already highly bookmarked)

Key Features of Delicious Blogs

1 – Powerful Headlines and Titles

Some readers will bookmark a page without even reading it, on the basis of an intriguing or tantalising title. When your post gets to Delicious, its title will entice others to click through, if it stands out enough to get their attention.

2 – Lists

Lists are *easy to scan* and readers don't have to waste their precious time trawling through dense, off-putting paragraphs. *Numbered lists* (e.g. Top 10 most stupid-looking URLs, Top 10 Online Darwin Awards etc) also work well.

3 – Widgets which Encourage Bookmarking

Social media optimization: Make your blog post easy to bookmark by including bookmarking icons or links and encouraging your regular visitors to bookmark, or vote for your post on social websites. Besides importing contacts from other networks, you can go to the Settings page and click on 'Network Badges'. This will give you HTML code for your site or blog for easy network-joining.

Bookmark seeding is getting people you know to give your article a push by bookmarking it on their Delicious accounts. Usually multiple bookmarks (at least 15) are needed before your article starts to be noticed. Ask some of your friends to give your blog post an initial boost by bookmarking it. This artificially inflation of bookmarks is limited to your online social network. Don't spend too much time aggressively bookmark seeding; the returns are usually higher if you focus on writing quality content.

4 – Popularity on other social media sites

Try Digg, Stumbleupon, Technorati and Reddit. They are all gateways to each other.

There's no use following 'how to make your blog popular on Delicious' guides if the content of your blog isn't engaging enough to attract at least a few links/a bit of traffic in its own right – Without SEO strategies.

Try and answer these questions:

- What makes someone bookmark a specific article?
- What makes the visitor decide to save a link so as to revisit a webpage at a later stage? Remember: **Quality content is a prerequisite for success.**

3) Look What We've StumbleUpon

StumbleUpon is a <u>social bookmarking</u> site that is driven by a community of users who share links to online content (such as blog posts) they enjoy. StumbleUpon works using a simple voting system. Users submit links to content they want to share, which is called "stumbling". Other users can add their opinions to that stumbled content by giving it a "thumbs up" or a "thumbs down" using the StumbleUpon toolbar.

The Benefits of StumbleUpon:
StumbleUpon is easy to use and has the potential to drive a lot of traffic to your blog in the long term if one of your submitted blog posts picks up a lot of stumbles. It's also a great place to find new blogs or blog post ideas as well as to network with other bloggers.

5 Tips to Increase Blog Traffic with StumbleUpon

StumbleUpon is a great tool to <u>drive blog traffic</u>, but there are rules to follow to actually get positive results. Use the five StumbleUpon tips below to give your blog a traffic boost.

1. Don't Stumble Your Own Content
It's an unwritten rule of StumbleUpon that you should avoid stumbling your own content. Of course, that doesn't mean you can never submit your own content, but it's always better if someone else submits your content first. If you only stumble your own content, then other users may feel that you don't add any value to the StumbleUpon community aside from self-promotion.

2. Stumble a Variety of Content from a Variety of Sources
Take the time to stumble content from a variety of blogs and websites as well as a mixture of articles, photos and videos. Only stumble the very best content that you truly want to share with other StumbleUpon users. Avoid content that doesn't add value to others.

3. Use Great Titles and Descriptions

When you stumble content, take the time to write a great title and description for that content to entice other users to click through and view your submission. Vague titles and descriptions are not helpful to other users.

4. Make Friends

Take some time to get to know other members of the StumbleUpon community and befriend them. Your StumbleUpon presence will grow as you network with more users. Don't just add a friend then forget about them. The power of StumbleUpon grows the more you network.

5. Use One Account and One Identity

Don't try to fool the StumbleUpon community by creating multiple accounts or stumbling only your friends' content and vice versa. Chances are you'll get caught, which could lead to your content getting buried (sandboxed) or you getting banned from StumbleUpon temporarily or permanently. Follow the rules (even the unwritten ones).

> **WARNING: over-promoting your website using social bookmarking sites and other forms of social media can put you in the Google-Sandbox**
> The Google-sandbox is a phenomenon whereby pages which are excessively or unscrupulously search-engine optimized get pushed down in Google rankings to the point where they may as well disappear entirely. While the existence of the sandbox is debatable, be wary of techniques which could cause Google to penalize you – as this would be counterproductive to all of your search engine, social networking, and bookmarking strategies!

Ready to embark on the next stage of your web marketing strategy? Through social networking you can use personal connections and dialogues to promote your business. It's simple, cost-effective and enables you to reach millions of potential customers online. If used correctly, Social networks can build your web presence, attract interest in who you are, and what your company is about, and ultimately drive business to your website and that translates into sales.

Chapter 10: Public Relations, Press Releases & Publicity, Publicity, Publicity

PR Demystified – Using the <u>Media</u> to Market your Business

Public relations (PR) is the practice of managing the flow of information between a business, the media and the public. Almost every business or organisation interested in how it is portrayed in public will employ some level of PR.

Effective and pro-active PR will give your small business wider exposure in the marketplace. It's used in business marketing campaigns for a simple reason: the more people that hear of your business, the more chance you'll have of generating leads and gaining future clients. And lead generation for your small business is why you're reading this book.

PR, done right, also allows you to position your business in the media the way you would like it to be perceived by potential clients: as the expert in your field.

Why a PR Campaign is a Great Move to Market YOUR Small Business

PR campaigns are fantastic for marketing small to medium sized services or professional businesses. Why?

- PR campaigns don't require a large marketing budget

- PR allows you to use third-party outlets to talk about your service, which gives you an aura of objective legitimacy, even endorsement. PR achieves this because everybody is more likely to believe what others say about you than what you say about yourself. It's the same argument as to why testimonials are so important
- PR builds a rapport between your business and your niche market. It is an important step in building a relationship of trust so that potential clients feel confident in committing to using your services

The Single Most Important Piece of Advice in this Chapter...

This book is all about lead generation – and so is our approach to PR. If it doesn't get more clients for your small business, why bother?

Yes, it's nice to see your name in the paper, knowing all your friends will read it or hear about it. And that the cool guy from school who you lusted after will now realise their mistake in not inviting you to the Year 10 formal! But people read or listen to something about you and then forget—we all see many hundreds of messages a day. So what have you achieved for your small business, with 10 or even a 100 direct competitors all competing for mind space?

That's what makes small business PR so different: that raising your profile through the media or any other way has limited benefits, it is not a valuable outcome for a small business (see Chapter one for more analysis of this).

What you need is for the reader or viewer to have a reason to go to your website or to call an 1800 number. And the obvious reason is to get more information, to learn more about the topic. In short, to get the free gift of a White Paper or your newsletter. Now remember, journalists usually don't like sales people and certainly don't want to be seen to be in any way, shape or form promoting your business. So you need to disguise any benefit to yourself, and make sure the audience gets real value from the download.

What you need to say to the journalist who's about to interview has the benefit of being true—and if its not, maybe you should take a long hard look at your White Paper?

> "Sue, this is a complex issue and we've written an e-book that explains it in more detail. We are happy to make this available to your readers – they just have to go to:
> www.leadcreation.com.au/about/whitepaper."

Now, most will say OK, though sometimes government owned or more left wing media will go into their, "That's against our policy" speech.

If they do, you can compromise 'on the run' by sacrificing the capture of their details—you will still get the traffic (good for SEO) and some will like what they see and subscribe or contact you.

So you say something like: "Sue, it's not a problem. When they visit the page they are able to download the Paper without registering. And as you can see, (showing her) the report is full of information and is not at all salesy (if it is, maybe you should be selling "a set of steak knives with that"! Fix it!) We wrote it to be really informative so that they see us as the experts and so might call us one day if they have a need."

If they still say no, you may not want to give them too much of your valuable time. It's not worth it, as you will just be tomorrow's fish wrapper as my granny used to say.

Know Thy Target Audience or Die

It is <u>fundamental</u> to an effective and powerful PR campaign that you know who your niche market is <u>before</u> you start. If your target market is 'everyone', you are casting your net too wide and your limited marketing budget will be wasted. If you narrow your focus, however, to target a single niche then you can direct your advertising and promotions to where this specific group congregates, to what they read, to what websites they go to and so on. **You can only ever effectively reach a niche (as we showed in Chapter one).**

Consider the following questions so that you can properly target your PR efforts to your niche:

- Who is your ideal customer?
- Where do you want to generate leads?
- What age group do they fall under?
- What magazines/newspapers do they read?
- What TV shows do they watch?
- What websites do they visit?
- What radio shows do they listen to?
- What social networks are they on? LinkedIn, Twitter, Stumbleupon, etc.
- What are their hopes and aspirations?
- What do they fear?
- What are their interests and hobbies?
- Where do the like to spend their money?
- How much do they earn?
- Who are your main competitors for this market?

There's no point attempting to get stories into publications that your target market, your Gold Clients, simply don't read. And remember, your target market isn't 'everyone'. By marketing to everyone, you won't reach <u>anyone</u> because your messages will be too diffused. Once you work out exactly who you want to appeal to and where you want to generate leads, you'll begin developing the messages that are going to make them specifically sit up and take notice whenever your small business is featured in the media. You have to *target* your PR campaigns in order to get results—small business marketers can't afford to do anything else.

Advertising Small Businesses for Free with PR

A press release is free advertising for your small business. It is also a commonly used and valuable way for the media, and subsequently the public, to be made aware of your news, new products and services. A tightly focused PR campaign can be very cost effective and long lasting. Why do a one-off marketing promotion when you could implement a free publicity campaign and have ongoing results? **Ongoing** lead generation for your small business—magic!

Generating publicity has several unique benefits that advertising simply doesn't have.

Firstly, it's free. With PR money doesn't change hands, which is rather cost-effective. What we're talking about here is the difference between getting your product/service talked about on a news or a current affairs program (in a positive light) *versus* the cost of producing an ad and buying time or space to run it. Both methods get your service on TV or radio, but one you paid for and one you didn't. And potential customers are more likely to be interested in the free one!

Secondly, PR gives your small business credibility. Consumers know when they see an ad that a company has produced it to say favorable things about their own products and services. They know the intent behind it is to get them to part with their cash. When they see a business, product or service talked about in the media however, they don't instantly make these assumptions. They're more likely to be receptive to your company if it's presented by a third party.

Thirdly, PR can position you as The Expert. If you get interviewed by the media as a representative of your field, you've instantly been cast as The Expert, someone who needs to be listened to. This is credibility that will encourage potential clients to trust you and respect your opinion. Increased media exposure generates increased sales. However, that's only the beginning, because publicity builds on itself and increases over time if you follow some simple steps.

Lastly, it's easy and anyone can do it. Anyone can get publicity for their company if they know the rules to the game being played. You just need to follow a tried and tested formula. And that's what this chapter will reveal to you—you'll learn how simply and effectively a PR campaign can be run.

PR's Six Golden Rules to Success

1. **Keep a constant eye out for media opportunities** – they are literally everywhere, all the time, and you will learn to spot them. Aim to make publicity a regular part of your marketing.

2. **Go for the easiest PR opportunities first** – if you've never done an interview before, don't attempt to get yourself straight into the hot seat on a high rating current affairs show. Aim for a local paper or radio station first—they are more likely be interested in the *'stories I'm trying out on the media to learn about how PR works'* anyway. Work on your interview performance with these opportunities <u>first</u> before you attempt the 'big time'.

3. **Know what you want to achieve before you start** – Tailor your story to suit the particular radio stations, TV shows or papers that your target market reads. There's no point getting your story out to an audience who are never going to buy your service because it's irrelevant to them. Or to places your small business can't deliver its service—internet marketing <u>and</u> PR

can be tailored to reach the local audiences of a typical small business.

4. **Seize upon topical stories of the day** – whatever is popular news right now is what you want to get a press release out on. <u>Now</u>. Tying your business or product to a hot topic in some way, even tenuously, will greatly improve your publicity and sales.

5. **Create a story relevant to topics that are simply <u>always</u> in the news** – When was the last time you saw a story about how to save money, Iraq, reduce credit card debt, bad drivers, immigration, a fad diet, what foods are good or bad for you, assessing the security of your home? The answer is almost every day (boring and even pathetic, but true!). Working out a way to link your products and services to recurrent discussion questions will help generate PR for your small business or SME.

6. **Make your story relevant to upcoming holidays or a particular 'international day' of something** – When a public holiday or an event like Valentine's, Red Nose Day or Earth Hour comes up, there are always numerous stories about it in the news. Work out an angle to link your small business to one of these events and watch some new clients roll through your doors (well, after they downloaded your White Paper!).

Your Company's Stories = Newsworthy Topics

It's all about the angle you take and the way you tell the story. By emphasising different factors in your story you'll make it more appealing to journalists and to different media. Things you need to concentrate on are:

- **Novelty Factor** – is there something new, different or quirky about your product/service/small business you can discuss that will be interesting to the general public?

- **Instruction Value** – everybody loves a 'How-To' guide. They are seen to present valuable advice in an easy to understand format. Creating a 'Seven Steps to...' guide and offering it for free on radio/TV programs will definitely get publicity.

- **Speak up, Speak out** – Controversy is always news. We're not talking the kind of controversy that might land you in the lockup, but rather if you have an opposite view to what others are saying in the media, speak up! Make sure you have the facts to back you up. Passion and controversy quickly generate interest and publicity.

- **Human Interest** – Do you have a story to tell that involves poverty to riches, overcoming great odds, or someone downtrodden who deserves better? The trashy popular press just loves these!

  Perhaps a client benefited immensely from your work, or your small business lent a hand to someone in a time of need? Most trade publications won't be interested in these stories, but mainstream, populist media loves them.

- **Uniqueness** – Is your company doing things differently to the majority? Can you make real, measurable differences to your clients—above and beyond what your competitors are doing? Someone, somewhere in the media wants to know about it. And is desperate to fill that yawning white space!

Why Would a Journo Be Interested at all?

The truth is that journalists are human beings who have a job to do just like anyone else. Every day pressure is on with targets to achieve and deadlines to meet. Investigative journalism takes time and doesn't generate continuous stories along the way to that big, breaking story. Journalists simply can't be researching, chasing up sources and interviewing all the time because the reality is they've got column space to fill. They are under constant pressure to have stories ready for the next issue. And the next.

And some days are simply 'slow news days'. Media professionals always run into the problem of what to write about next, and if you can pitch your story to them in a way that shows it as a relevant, interesting, topical and newsworthy story, more often than not they're happy to hear from you. And the way you 'pitch' to the media is via a 'press release'.

A press release is a one or two page document with a particular layout and structure that is sent to a journalist to alert them about a potential story topic. Be aware that journalists and editors receive press releases in their hundreds every day, but there are ways to make yours stand out and you will learn them in this chapter. But remember, it is a skill to write a press release that captures a journalist's (and later the public's) imagination and attention. It is a skill that takes practice, but is very valuable and you won't forget it when it starts to generate leads for your small business.

Your Press Release – How, What, When, Who, Why?

Creating a 'Leap From the Pile' Press Release

Many stories in the paper, on the radio and on the six o'clock news are generated from press releases—probably far more than you think. The 'free to air' media is under huge cost pressures and they have less and less journalists to dig out stories in this world of bloggers, social media and pay TV. The key to gaining media attention is to craft a great story, and you *do* have a story to tell even if you think your business is boring. You just have to find the right angle and convey it well. You'll know you've grabbed the media's attention when you get the call wanting to know more. So how do you achieve it?

Finding and Developing Your Story

To unearth some of your own stories, ask yourself:

- What's different about my business, staff, product/service?
- What's different about my staff policy or the way I run the business?
- Do any of my personal beliefs or philosophies impact on my business?
- Why do I do what I do?
- How does my service make people's lives easier or better?
- How and why and where did I get started? Do you have a 'started in my garage' story?
- What facts or research prove the need for my new service?
- Why do people like working for my small business?
- What obstacles have I overcome to get where I am today? (Being boring is an obstacle, but not newsworthy! OK, that was an attempted joke.)
- Is my life story unique/interesting (e.g. child of migrant parents; grandparents from 4 different countries; lived in 5 countries as I grew up; arrived on a leaky boat)?
- Does my business help the community in some way?
- Is my new service or product the result of a 'lucky accident', arose from serendipity?
- Is my business based on an old family secret?
- Did something I learned overseas influence my business?
- Is my product environmentally friendly? Can it be seen from a positive green angle?
- Is my service cheaper/more expensive than others' products and why?
- What passions of mine drive me in my business life?

The emphasis in most of the questions you asked was on 'what's different' and what makes you unique. Exploring the answers to these diverse questions could result in a great story. Or at least some interesting content to refer to in the story.

If you put in years of hard work and dedication, fought against the odds, experienced something terrible and knew things had to change, had a dream, a lucky accident, stumbled upon something no one had ever thought of before, had a bolt of inspiration that caused you to create something innovative that filled a gap in the market—this is interesting stuff. This is <u>newsworthy</u> stuff that the media would love to hear about.

The funny thing is, when I wrote down my own answers to those questions I was truly amazed. They <u>really</u> looked interesting. It's human nature to think that our story is mundane because it's what we know, we are too close to it. But it rarely is.

Any of these ideas could be the basis for your story about your small business. Think about content that is engaging and possibly a bit unusual, and there's your story waiting to be written. If you write down the answers to these questions and keep them handy for whenever you want to write a new press release, it'll make your job a many times easier.

Before You Write, What's Your Angle?

There are literally hundreds of ways you could write any particular story. If I told you to write something 'about Iraq', you might take any number of different slants to discuss this topic. Depending upon your particular profession, business and life history, you could end up with a number of completely different stories. With completely different angles. For example, I might write about how small business internet marketing is different in a war zone! How the constant danger of being blown up by misguided fundamentalists changes what you need to do in your marketing. I'll ponder that and think of some examples for our second edition—and no, I am not trivializing it. It is a constant and ongoing tragedy that we have created by invading Iraq. But businesses still need to survive, life still goes on.

What angle you take is up to you, but remember that the following are **aspects that make your story newsworthy**:

- A response (or opposite response) to a story already in the news
- Controversy
- Facts
- Curiosity factor
- Human interest story – it is always what drives the media. Add good pictures and your story is up and running!
- Good Samaritanism – too rare, but a lot of human interest as we all want there to be more of it
- A problem solved
- Time or money savings now possible with new technology, demographic changes or whatever
- Showing how a tragedy or a great waste could have been prevented with your service/product
- Health benefits

To pick the angle for your story, imagine that your release is being written for your 'gold client' and them alone. What are they interested in, what do they want to hear about from your small business?

But is this <u>Really</u> a Newsworthy Story?

Not all stories are the investigative journalism type that change the way society views something or someone in a prominent position or is enjoying their 15 minutes of fame. Some news stories are simply topical information of interest to a specific sector of society. The key to a 'newsworthy' story is to arouse curiosity.

In the PR world it pays to be a bit over the top and to 'blow your own trumpet' to promote the products of your small business or SME. You need to draw attention to yourself, and engage people's desire to know more. In order to do this you should emphasise your **'points of difference'**. You already have points of difference from your competitors, things that make your business unique and something of a standout from the pack, you only need to point them out in an interesting way.

Your points of difference can be found amongst you or your employees' many life skills and experiences, or could be related to a unique way you manage your business. Maybe you have a creative work philosophy to motivate yourself and your staff. Maybe the fact that you've travelled extensively could be of interest to the media. Maybe you have 10 or 20 years experience doing something that somehow develops your credibility in a particular story. Maybe you grow your own vegetable garden or hang glide. Or like me, you ride a Vespa scooter with an orange flag waving on the back (for safety, not because I'm an exhibitionist! But I've never seen another one in any of the 20 cities I've visited in the last 5 years, so I guess it says something about me)

Your specific life skills and experiences will allow you to talk on diverse related topics with a far greater deal of authority. There are many points of difference about you and your small business once you start to scratch the surface. Differences that will generate the leads you are seeking.

To find them, write down a list of all the things you can do and have done in your small business, no matter how irrelevant or silly they may seem. Whenever you see an opportunity to use some of these details in a press release about yourself, your products, services or small business, you should use it. Including snippets like this increases your chances of getting a story into the news, because they establish you as a real and unique person, and someone who is a bit of a character—ultimately, someone who people would be interested in reading about and meeting. You'll simply and effectively establish yourself as someone who'd make a good story because you have some interesting 'points of difference'.

Making Your Press Release Count

First Things First – The Headline

Your headline must demand: **"Read Me Now!"** The headline is the crucial element in getting your release read and considered for a story. Your headline should be catchy and grab the attention of whoever reads it, and make them want to read more. A headline is the ad for your press release. If your headline is great then it has a strong chance of becoming a news item, whereas a great release with a poor headline will most likely end up in the bin. Tough, but true. Media professionals may see 100 or more press releases everyday, and if the headline doesn't catch their attention then they won't waste time trying to work out whether the content's any good.

In order to work out what a good headline is, pay attention to headlines that catch your attention and draw you to read when you next make your way through the paper. You'll notice that these headlines never give away the full story, and prompt you to guess a bit about what the content of the article will be.

This is what you want to do with your headlines—arouse curiosity and intrigue, and to draw people into seeking more information. Also look at headlines that utterly bore you and don't make you want to read on. What is it about them that doesn't work? Avoid these mistakes in your own work. Learning opportunities for PR are everywhere in the media, so take advantage of them.

An easy way to develop your headline is to consider the most important keywords from your press release and attempt to word them in a really engaging, curiosity arousing way. An outrageous, intriguing or thought provoking statement can work wonders. You may also communicate your strongest benefit if the story is about your product or service. Your headline should appeal to your target audience's self-interest and a good headline always addresses the question 'What's in it for me?' for your target audience.

Here are 9 Simple Steps to Your Perfect Headline

1. Find your basic story
2. Choose 10 or 20 background facts
3. Decide on your angle
4. Write the bare facts of your story
5. Write a headline and consider is it interesting and intriguing?
6. Breakdown each fact into background facts
7. Include descriptive, powerful, emotive, feeling words
8. Re-write your headline
9. Does your headline pass the "Who Cares" Test? Is it interesting, provoke curiosity, make you want to find out more, is it easy to read and understand and above all does it make sense?

Ted Nicholas is a direct marketing guru, self-made copywriting millionaire and a great guy to hang out with (he now lives in Switzerland, he is formerly from the USA). These are his favourite words to use in headlines to arouse interest and curiosity. Use them creatively – they're great.

Ted Nicholas' 27 Favourite & Most Effective Headline Words:

1. Announcing
2. Secrets of (rebellious entrepreneurs revealed)
3. New
4. Now
5. Amazing
6. Facts you should know about
7. Breakthrough
8. At last
9. Advice to
10. The truth of
11. Protect
12. Life (will not be the same as a result of)
13. Here
14. Discover
15. Do you
16. Bargains
17. Yes ("Yes Toby, I can't wait another moment, please deliver")
18. Love
19. Hate (Don't hate yourself for missing out)
20. How much
21. How would
22. This
23. Only (way left for the little guy to get ahead)
24. Sale
25. Free
26. You (don't use 'me')
27. How to

The Art of the Tease – Getting <u>Them</u> to Call <u>You</u>

There's no point writing a release that neatly sums up your entire story. If you do the journalist can write the story without you and probably won't need to mention your small business. The goal in your release is to get their attention and whet their appetite. You want to get the journalist, producer or reader curious for more details. If you get a call back you're far more likely to get a better article or more time on air, rather than a small story that barely has time to interest your potential customer before they've moved on to the next thing.

So don't give the whole story—instead, hint at things or offer tantalising bits of information that prompt intrigue. Your offer for them to contact and interview you gives them an avenue to find out more details, and a further opportunity for you to promote your product/service/business.

You should always apply the 'So what? Who cares? Test' to your press release as you would do in all lead generation activities—the media are like 'leads' for your small business, they are 'prospects' but with a difference. If the release is filled with interesting, colourful facts and isn't boring and dull, it passes the test. If it makes you want to find out more, then it passes the test. Make sure you're honest with your facts or get someone unbiased to have a look at it and tell you if you're too close to read it objectively. Once your release passes 'the test', the media are that much more likely to jump onto the phone to you. Now that's lead generation!

What Does a Press Release Look Like?
Here's Your Template

PRESS RELEASE for immediate release (Just PRESS RELEASE if it's not time sensitive)
Sydney, December 2009 *(or you can specify a date for release e.g. near Australia Day or Thanksgiving if your story was relevant to that.)*

Headline to Rock Socks off Journos – Grab Attention, Arouse Interest, Curiosity and Intrigue. Specific and Newsworthy!

Paragraph One will follow on from your headline and tell the full story without revealing the details. Set the scene. Focus on what is the actual news; why is this news? The people, products, items, dates and other things related to this news; the purpose behind the news; your company – the source of the news. You want to demonstrate the newsworthiness of your story. Sum up the entire story quickly here. Write in the third person throughout and keep the release as clear, simple and short as possible. Basic language is fine. Write as a journalist would—read up on your main target media outlets to get an idea of their style.

Paragraph Two should establish as much credibility as possible for your product, service and/or small business. It should contain facts that support the angle of your press release such as data from studies or surveys, quotes from happy customers, reviewers or an expert. It can also contain background information about you, your small business, your staff or product. But beware—don't fall into the trap of being 'salesy' or you'll lose the reader's interest. Journalists typically <u>hate</u> sales. They rightly don't see it as their job to sell or promote your business.

Paragraph Three should sum up your story and provide any last details or points that are important. You can mention here price and availability and perhaps link this release to topical events. Mention the reason why you are doing what you are doing and/or link the story to another currently in the news. Don't give it all away—leave your reader wanting more! Use the same press release for the local paper or a major TV show. The only time you change your release is if it isn't working. Make sure you edit your work, and preferably once you've written the release leave it for two days and check it again after that to see if it really passes the 'So what? Who cares? Test'. If it does, you're onto a winner.

END

(This is the typical way to end a release. If it is not used it might look like there was more to this release which got lost)

Include contact details in a separate box at the very bottom. Always mention, "if you would like an interview with <u>your name or contact person's name</u> please contact" so that the media knows you are available for interviews.

If you would like an interview with (<u>your name or name of contact person</u>), please contact:

Name or contact person's name
Phone   Email
Fax   Mobile

An Example of a *lead creation* Press Release

MEDIA RELEASE for immediate release
Sydney, November 12th, 2009

Why are Small Businesses falling prey
to the dodgiest of Salesmen?

The Truth about the Marketing Game and the 'Magic Pill' Myth

The equivalent of daylight robbery is happening to small and medium sized Australian businesses looking to improve their marketing in tough times. All small businesses know they need more clients to survive but their lack of knowledge about marketing leaves them defenceless to dodgy salesmen. These salesmen (usually) have a good product—nothing wrong with it. The problem is that they hard sell it as the 'Magic Pill', _the_ answer to growing a business. But in reality, they only sell a single and expensive piece of the marketing puzzle which cannot work in isolation.

Sydney based **lead creation** have a new book available on Amazon on November 12th. The book highlights how the marketing needs of small business are very different to big companies. They need to spend much less than big companies on each piece of marketing, and in most cases they should just tell the salesman to go talk to BHP or McDonalds.

Here's an example: a small business wants to attract new customers so they go to a marketing consultant. They get sold on the idea of advertising with a big, beautiful billboard...only to discover later that the billboard is standing opposite a semi-demolished building and a few dumpsters in a side alley where very few, if any, people go past each day. Great billboard + poor location = no new clients.

OK, so that wouldn't happen too often! But here's a story that happens hundreds of times a day—the equivalent of the invisible 'billboard' on line ...

The Web salesman persuades a business to build an expensive and pretty website. But that's <u>all</u> they sell, the website. They don't mention 'optimizing' the website, which is essential to make it visible online to potential new customers (what's called 'SEO'). And they ignore interactivity.

The problem with this for small business is that a website is useless if no one can find it, more so if you don't implement the three other elements necessary to make that website interactive. If your site's interactive you can start a conversation with the potential customers who have visited your site.

This is an all too common problem—a small business gets sold on one marketing element which in isolation cannot generate new customers and just eats up their scarce dollars. What they need is a diversification of strategy and to carefully spend <u>less</u> on each piece of the marketing puzzle. And to send the Magic Pill salesmen packing.

END

If you would like an interview with Toby Marshall, please contact:

Toby Marshall of *lead creation*   admin@leadcreation.com.au
+61 (02) 9281 5938   www.leadcreation.com.au

So You've Crafted Your Fantastic, Standout Press Release. Now What?

If you want a spot on a radio or television program, you need to send your release directly to the show's producer. If you're looking to get your story in print media such as newspapers or magazines or a popular Blog, you need to send your release directly to the editor. Whoever you're sending it to, make sure you spell their name correctly!

Concentrate your efforts on impressing the right person, the one who has control over the content on a show or paper that your target market watches or reads. And remember, no publicity effort is too small for a small business or SME because stories that feature in the local paper occasionally get picked up and run in other media. But also, it is very focused media and so is higher value—customers like to buy local which is sometimes forgotten in the world of internet marketing and Web 2.5. Talkback radio is often far more likely to interview newcomers to the publicity circuit than bigger, network stations. This is often a stepping stone process. PR starts out small and builds and builds.

Always be on the lookout for publicity opportunities you can tie a story in on and keep tuned to what kind of angles in stories make them newsworthy. Read your papers, magazines, online news sites, listen to radio and talkback, and watch the news as much as you can. You'll know the various interview styles of different media this way and be prepared for them if they ever interview you. This will also help you pick up tips as to how the person being interviewed promotes their own business, products and services. Considering all this, thinking about what went on behind the scenes to get a person in the news/on TV will make you realise just how many news stories were generated by a press release.

How and Where do you Send Your Releases?

You can send your releases out to the media in a number of ways. Choose the option that best suits your purpose and go with it.

You might send your releases:

- To relevant, specific publications/shows by finding out the contact details **through Media Guides and Directories**
- **Through the Australian Associated Press (AAP) in Australia. There will be similar services in other countries.** To do this you'll need to pay to become a member, however, this is an extremely fast and efficient way of targeting numerous media outlets. Their lists are also accurate and up-to-date it, and is low cost. At *lead creation* we use it for our internet marketing business. Your release will also be placed on the AAP website which some journalists search in order to find stories.
- **To specific journalists, editors and producers** working on publications and shows your target audience consumes
- **To a list of journalists who've run your stories before.** This is your gold list, your exciting customers. Marketing gold lies in your clients- generating leads is vital, but never as profitable as 'mining' your exciting clients (or journalists)

Publicity is <u>not</u> a one off event, but rather something that builds and grows. There are two actions you can take to encourage this growth. Firstly, keep a record of whom you have contacted in the past, their contact details, if and when your story ran, and any other comments you might like to add. If you had a good interview with them and got along well, you might add them onto your shortlist of journalists to send releases to. They're likely to remember you and be favourable to running another of your stories again rather than talk to someone who they've never met or heard of before. You can also use this record to track which kinds of media exposure, got you the most sales or new customers, and you can target your future PR efforts to what media was most effective.

Secondly, it doesn't hurt to send out a Thank You letter (the stamp and envelope kind) after you've sent your release, whether it was used or not. If you sent the release to hundreds of outlets, you don't have to do this. But if you're only sending to ten or so who work for very targeted publications/programs that are relevant to your company, why wouldn't you? You only need to send a short note to thank them for their time, and for considering your article or for running your article if they did so. The chances are most journalists, editors or producers won't have received a letter like this before, or at least very rarely, and so it will stand out to them.

Most people who send out releases take it for granted that journalists will or won't run a story and that that is all there is to it. Finito. However small, courteous touches go a long way to making journalists look more favourably on your PR, both now and in the future. Developing relationships with media personnel is an important part of PR. Relationships are important in all small business marketing and all lead generation of course, both offline and online.

Before you get The Call from the Interviewer

You must be ready for the media attention once it comes and make the most of it. You may get a call 10 minutes after you've sent your release out where a journalist wants to interview you right there and then. My record was five minutes! You need to be prepared so that you don't get caught on the spot. If a journalist is really interested in your story, then they're going to want all the details ASAP. Be prepared to give it to them so they don't lose interest while you flounder around trying to get your stuff in order.

Before you send out your release, you should have prepared a **background page** ready to send to an interviewer so that they can gather a bit more information on you for their story. These are your details that show a more human and personal side to the journalist so that they have some interesting background to include about you in their article.

Your background page should include:

- When/how your small business started
- Any good deeds/community service your company provides
- Some of your major achievements such as winning awards or big contracts
- What's innovative or different about you and/or your staff
- Any interesting hobbies you or your staff have
- Any instance when your small business was an industry leader or the first to do something (and can be just first in your region or town—that's news to the local paper)
- The story behind why you chose to create or invent a new product or service

Along with your background page, you may need to email/fax/mail some (flattering) pictures of your workplace or yourself if required. Find some appropriate and professional ones. A good photo is one that's adequately lit, in focus and has lots of pixels. And if you have a photo of yourself with a dog, all the better! Apparently individuals trust people with dogs more, as it shows a caring, human side to them. My dog is about to become a media star! However, whatever you go with, choose a professional picture that best suits your story.

The Real Deal: the "We'd like to do a Story on *You*" Call

When the journalist calls to interview you, here is your checklist:

- First and foremost: if you don't already know, check who the audience of the program/paper is. Ask for the approximate size of the audience, their location and their demographics. Now you may find this hard to believe, but you might want to refuse the interview if it is not your audience. Your time is valuable, whether you want to be interviewed is up to you. Of course, say no politely and explain why.
- Ask for the angle of the story—this is vital so you know how to frame your answers to make them more relevant and so more likely to get you in the media

  *Now, those 2 questions have another **huge** benefit: you get a little breathing space before they start firing questions at you. And believe me, time to take a few deep breaths get your head clear is <u>always</u> valuable.*

- Ask when the story will be broadcast or printed
- Set aside enough time for your interview – check with the interviewer as to the likely length
- Ask to get a copy of the audio/video/magazine/newspaper you'll appear in—it can be hard to get a clean copy later. And you'll need it to send to all the people you know, 90% of whom will not have seen or heard it
- Ask whether they were thinking a live or recorded interview if it's to go on TV or radio—recorded is a <u>lot</u> easier on your stress levels!

- Practice what you want to say and get across just before you send the release out
- Offer to send through the link to your background page (or attach it)
- Have some water handy to moisten your throat
- Have your calendar ready to organise a time if now doesn't suit either of you. And if you are not ready and need more time, it doesn't reflect badly on you—looking busy is always good. Plus unless it is a real breaking story and they are on deadline, you can usually call them back at a time when you are ready (however <u>always</u> ask the two audience/angle questions before you hang up)
- Have an **interview 'prompt sheet'** you've prepared earlier in front of you with your major points on it in case you get stuck – this contains <u>facts, figures, quotes, studies, testimonials</u> and so on. It's amazing how stuff you know really well vanishes under pressure. The mind just goes mushy and sometimes completely blank—it's happened to me!
- Be in a quiet, private area—move if you're not, and know in advance where you'll go. You cannot give a good interview if its noisy and people are listening in
- Be mentally prepared and understand what the media is looking for
- Speak slowly and clearly
- Use humor, be passionate about your topic, don't swear
- Talk about the benefits your product/service/small business generates for others
- Keep your goal in mind
- Be ready to show TV crews/photographers around your business. It surprised me when this first happened to me, but in hindsight I can see why. It provides some color and helps position you as a real person

- Be ready to travel to a radio or TV studio—and be prepared to hang around a lot (I take my iphone so can email and text, plus always take some reading I need to catch up on and isn't too heavy as there are often interruptions)
- Only reveal things you're happy to have 'on the record'. A journalist may ask a question you hadn't considered or ask something personal. Keep your interview focused on the story you want to tell. Politely change the subject or do what all politicians do: answer the question you want to answer!
- Get your important points across and realise that your content will definitely be edited
- If you have to travel to get to the interview for a TV program, consider asking them to pay for your expenses. However, don't make this a deal breaker. Think of the free advertising, and sales you'll make from the publicity instead.
- Look professional when you're interviewed face-to-face
- Relax, speak naturally and try to enjoy the experience. It's a fantastic opportunity! And it is not the be-all and end-all opportunity. Follow our formula and there will be many more

The more time and effort you put into preparing for the media, the more confident and relaxed you'll be during the interview. You will be clearer and get your point across more directly. And once you've prepared your background page, you can use it every time someone calls to interview you. And remember, everyone is nervous the first time, particularly people in small business. The media is used to it. Don't apologise for it. Don't draw attention to it.

How Much Publicity is Enough Publicity?

How long is a piece of string? The more publicity you want, the more media outlets you should be sending your releases out to. However, consider how many interviews you can handle and what you're attempting to achieve with a particular press release. If you want to link your story to a local community event where your small business is located, you won't want to be targeting national newspapers or radio stations, but rather <u>local</u> and community papers and radio stations.

You should tailor your PR efforts in order to suit your specific aims and situation. This can become easy to forget in the excitement of sending releases out and waiting hopefully for the phone to ring. Make sure you only target relevant media for each story. You only want your story told in publications where your niche market is—the Gold Clients that are the focus of your small business marketing.

As mentioned earlier, publicity is <u>not</u> a one off event. It's a process and it is ongoing. PR campaigns can be used over and over to gain free advertising. Each campaign will teach you something new about the process and will hone your skills. Like all skills worth acquiring it takes practice and as my Gran used to say, practice makes perfect (loved her dearly, but her clichés could get a bit annoying!).

Sometimes you will need to rewrite releases because they weren't effective, or you'll get a call for an interview but then the story will be bumped because something more interesting came up.

In Mid 2009, I had a major nine minute story on Australia's premier current affairs show, the 7:30 Report. It got bumped twice due to the first cabinet reshuffle of the newish Australian prime minister—it finally ran on the third day. Don't be disheartened. It happens. Our point is that the more campaigns you run, the more times you'll get your name out there in the media and out amongst your target market. So don't hold back and don't give up!

PR can do amazing things. It can generate large amounts of interest, new customers/clients and sales—it's the perfect lead generation tool for small business without much money to invest. That said, be prepared for the onslaught once your campaign succeeds, maintain your focus on what you want to promote, and really use every opportunity you can in order to get your product/service/company and story out there into the media. Your small business and your team will love you for it. Why not kick-start the PR process today?

Chapter 11: Referrals—How to get More for your Small Business

Your Clear-Cut How-To Guide to Getting Referrals

Referrals are valued by businesses, for two main reasons:

1. The cost of your sales process is reduced

2. The relationship starts with a level of trust, with your small business "well positioned"

To obtain anything of value (such as referrals), there are three golden rules. You need to:

1. Have a plan

2. Ask for what you want

3. Make it easy for people to help you get it

Referrals from Existing Clients – Just Ask!

You have been doing everything right. Your client is happy. Their needs are being met — so what's going on, why aren't they referring you?

Firstly, keep in mind that you are dealing with very busy (and most likely self-absorbed) people and companies. It comes as no surprise, then, that <u>your</u> wants and needs are the least of their concerns. You need to take the initiative and ask them. Success does not come easily – don't be afraid of rejection or that they don't follow through, it happens. Pick yourself up and move along to the next—persevere.

People will often talk positively about their service providers, but they won't be inclined to refer them <u>unless</u> they are asked. As a last resort, however, you may want to try enticing clients with incentives. Everybody loves incentives. Whether it be discounts, free upgrades and services or even a small thank you gift. But not something so valuable that it will be seen as a bribe, so usually give more of your product. A plasma TV will rightly be seen as a bribe, not an incentive.

If you're finding you are not getting anywhere, you may need to revaluate your position. Have you earned the right to ask for a referral in the first place? Is your service worth it?

Make it Easy for your Clients

What is always the key ingredient for establishing and maintaining a healthy relationship with other people? The answer is always better communication.

One way to communicate is to make sure your clients get the inside scoop via regular newsletters— it's easy and cost effective. The content of these newsletters should educate clients about new goods and services or simply the latest news. They should also have some personal news and even contain some fun or humour.

Regular newsletters will benefit you by implicitly reminding your existing clients about your business and what it can bring to the table. In the long run, it will also make it easier for them to publicise your business. A brief statement about your business objectives, goods and services as well as benefits is another great promotional tool. Even just a few key words to summarise your position will come in handy. You may even want to create a detailed brochure or write a witty, yet informing article. Lastly, if you do not have a website—create one. If you have a website, update it regularly and refer your clients to it.

Now, although this is all important, let's reverse this 'me, me, me' mentality for a moment and turn our focus to the clients. What do you know about them? It is important to keep an up-to-date database about your clients and potential clients. By following this two way interaction model, you will create and generate referrals.

The Big Tip...

Ask for a referral immediately that you are awarded the contract or the order. The following way of asking has nearly a 100% success rate:

> *Thanks for the contract; we are looking forward to ('doing a great job') for you. When as expected we have delivered and you are happy with the results, we would then really appreciate two things from you.*

> *Firstly, a testimonial about our work, and secondly we'd like to ask for the names of others you know who might also benefit from our service.*

So, you are getting permission and also creating a slight obligation to do what they agreed to when you later ask for these two small but extremely valuable favors.

When you have completed the work and are doing your "post project feedback" session, ideally face to face, is the best time to ask. It's also helpful to ensure you have allowed enough time as it can take a while for them to think of some referrals.

Now you need to make it easy for them – you need to be <u>very</u> clear about the clients you are seeking more of. How you describe them must be succinct, meaningful and actionable by your client.

To illustrate, at our business *lead creation*, we say:

> *The clients we can most help are small businesses in Professional Services or Business to Business sales who provide a great service but not enough people know about what they offer and the value they provide – so they need to raise their profile both online and offline. They typically have less than 100 staff and could be as small as just the owner. And most importantly, many don't have a lot of spare cash at the moment so our low fees are well regarded.*

Then we give them prompts to help them – you can even show them a list. *lead creation*, has the following types of organisations on our list:

Financial Planners

Accountants

Lawyers

Engineering Consultants

Stock Brokers

Project Managers

Strategic Consultants

HR Consultants

Recruitment Firms

Business Coaches

Executive Coaches

Life Coaches

Training Companies

© www.leadcreation.com.au

Architects

Non-Executive Directors

Quantity Surveyors

Marketing and Branding Consultants

IT Companies

IT Support

Then you can ask a couple of prompting questions to dig out referrals, questions which will of course vary by business. For example:

- **What about the people who supply your business?**
- **People you know from your Golf club/children's schools/etc?**

If they are too busy right now or can't think of anyone, say something like, "Why don't I leave the list with you and give you a call next week". And ideally, you need to send them something between now and then (a free report, or a press article of interest) <u>without</u> reminding them of the referrals—the subtle, 'not so pushy' approach is best.

Worth all the effort? Absolutely. But really, it's not much of an effort if you remember to ask up front.

Referrals from Non-Clients

Let's look at getting referrals from people who are <u>not</u> clients. Follow a similar process to what we outlined above, which is to ask for it but always in a structured way. With non-clients there is also a case for using an incentive to encourage people to make an effort.

What we have found effective in our small business, *lead creation* is to offer three alternatives:

1. **A thousand dollars (5% to 10% of the price of our full marketing system with all 9 modules implemented)**
2. **A thousand dollars to a charity or association of their choice**
3. **To fix an element of their own marketing, one that will give them the most impact on their business.** For example, to choose from one of:

    i. To build a new, interactive website with a CMS

    ii. Get them on page one of Google search results

    iii. Set up their PR strategy to run in-house plus get one or two media articles published

    iv. Set up a Google AdWords campaign

Referrals are the best source of new business. To increase the amount you get, you need to focus on the <u>process</u> you follow—and in particular, to ask for them.

One-off marketing promotions <u>can</u> be effective, and are what most small business marketing consists of. But don't do a big marketing promotion <u>before</u> you have a customer reactivation program – it is always cheaper to reactivate existing customers than it is to get new ones. So running new promotions is good but not if you don't have a Referral Program in place – **referrals are the best new customers.**

To Get Referrals You Should...
Network, Network, Network!

We're not saying you need to be the life of the party, but at the very least make sure you're *at* the party. Show your face at one work related gathering a week, as this is a minimum requirement to get either referrals or new clients.

Next step—mingle. Events are a great opportunity to meet new prospects and make a lasting impression. Prior to attending these functions, it helps to research the likely attendees and what they do. Get to know about their business and their wants and needs. Offer your two cents and work on the all important 'care factor.' Implement the 'giving without hooks' concept. For example, offering counsel to someone who has confided a personal problem without expecting anything in return. This will help strengthen the dynamic and people will get to know, like and trust you.

Even before attending functions, perhaps it would be a wise idea to pinpoint possible gold clients or potential joint venture partners. Knowing the right people to mingle with is essential and will minimise wasting time on dead ends. Lastly, keep in the back of your head the five step ladder for turning a complete stranger into a close friend:

1. Suspects – People you have sussed out to have potential
2. Prospects – People who begin to show slight interest
3. Customers – People who use your product or service
4. Clients – Customer who have become loyal customers
5. Advocates – People who now promote your product or service

Listed below are places to start your referral chain:

- Trade associations
- Professional organisations
- Community service groups
- Religious groups
- Chambers of commerce
- Charities
- Groups specialised in referrals sharing

Also, think outside the box— or is it inside?

- Your suppliers
- Your friends
- Your vendors
- Your support services

Members of all of these groups, if asked, are likely to have one or two referrals.

Networking tools

Business cards. If you don't have them you're setting yourself up for failure as you are likely to be just another face, soon forgotten. A card acts as your silent salesperson—promoting your identity when you're not physically there to do it. Make sure, then, that you do it correctly. A business card firstly needs the obvious stuff: full name; company name; contact details including the area code with your phone number; what you do—your title, and if what you do is not clear from your title, change your title.

Now that's the bare minimum on the card. Some or all of the following are vital, and I use all of them (except the photo, the world doesn't need more ugliness):

- Make use of the back of your business card (products, services, objectives)
- Contact details on LinkedIn, Twitter
- Bilingual cards if necessary
- Coloured business cards
- Include a *professional* photograph

Post the Networking Event

You've networked. Now what? It's something many of us forget to do, but it is fundamental to maintaining your connections. You must **follow up.** While emailing or texting is OK, calling takes it a step further. Calling is more personal and shows you are making a genuine effort by taking time out of your schedule to build a relationship with them. It gives you the added qualities of creditability and portrays a professional image. It impresses. Good impressions lead to good referrals. Just don't try and sell anything on this first call. You wouldn't, would you?!

Lastly, remember to show your appreciation once you get a referral. You can do so by any of the following:

- Follow up call
- Thank you note/gift
- An email or a text (but that would be a 'not very valuable, don't want too many more' type of referral follow up
- Make them aware of any future success as a result of having received their referral

Social Networking

Social Networking is of course the most powerful tool. It has turbocharged our ability to network- see Chapter 9 for more on this world changing phenomena.

Referrals Take the Burden off You

Referrals will help you ensure the stability, profitability and growth of your small business into the future. You may even become a big business! 'Word of mouth'—friends telling their friends about your professional and effective service—is very cost-effective marketing. But in order to get more out of it than this, you need to turn happy customers into advocates who remember to go and tell their friends about you. Asking doesn't hurt, nor does developing a network of contacts who can mention you throughout their own extended networks.

Referrals mean that you get more out of one customer than just one or a few sales. You get that initial sale *plus* the number of friends they refer who also buy one or a few items. You are multiplying the value of your clientele. And it is simple to do. The strategies we've outlined in this chapter for you to employ to get more referrals will do just that, get more referrals—so take advantage of them

!

Chapter 12: Testimonials— The Most Powerful Tool for Building Your Business

Overcoming a Potential Client's Lack of Trust with Customer Testimonials

Customers today are way more savvy than when I entered the world of marketing nearly 40 years ago. Then the marketers were in control and we broadcast our message to the masses. We were telling and selling.

Today, just because you say your product or service is excellent, it doesn't mean they will believe you. In fact usually they won't, we are all a lot more skeptical.

In marketing a small business, it is not sufficient to simply proclaim that you are trustworthy and that you provide a valuable service, you need to provide proof. And every unsubstantiated claim you make is likely to be questioned by a prospective client before they part with their money. Even if you have <u>never</u> done a poor job, or would never dream of "ripping off" a client, your integrity will be questioned.

As one of my mentors in direct marketing used to say, "the loneliest place on the planet is the person sitting at their computer thinking of entering their credit card details" (thanks Mal—that's a great way to put it). Even if your clients don't pay by credit card, they still need help to get over the line, to make the decision to buy—they need to believe in your value.

So how can you prove your integrity to your prospects without sounding far-fetched? The most powerful solution is incredibly simple:

Provide testimonials from satisfied clients that you've worked for

It's a fundamental truth of marketing that potential clients will always find what others say about you <u>way</u> more believable that what you say about yourself. It is that simple. This is because most consumers know that you will promote and protect your own self interest above all else, so anything you say will be taken with a grain of salt. This is where the hierarchy of credibility comes into play, which we'll discuss later in the chapter.

What others say about your small business is more believable as their answer will more likely give a balanced view of the product or service you provide. Think of client testimonials as witnesses testifying about the value of your product or service in a courtroom—more believable than you if you are the defendant!

So because testimonials are so valuable in terms of marketing, getting them becomes an integral part of small business marketing (and particularly internet marketing). And the single key to getting testimonials is **to ask** for them. You'd be surprised how many happy clients are willing to do so if you simply ask.

In Marketing, it's all about Them, not You

In order to encourage new clients to trust you, you must avoid the common marketing mistake of adopting an ego-centric 'Me, Myself and I' mentality. What customers are really interested in (as we all are) is themselves, and not in you or anything you want to sell them. So accordingly, you need to shift the focus of your marketing away from yourself and your company, and onto your prospects—what *they* want and how they will greatly <u>benefit</u> through using your product. When you provide testimonials, you show the potential client that you've worked with people similar to them (because you've defined your niche), and have provided measurable and substantial benefits. You're giving evidence to prove your claims.

So, to change the focus of your marketing from you to them, you need to invest some time and energy into seeing things through the customers' eyes. How are they going to interpret what you say? Always assume a level of doubt from your prospect. You need to address any worries or objections a potential client may have when they first become aware of your products and services—and write these rebuttals directly into your copy. You need to make the prospect feel as comfortable as possible if they're going to commit to using your company. Good testimonials help you achieve this.

The Most Powerful Selling Weapon is Providing Proof that what you say is True

Marketing works when you successfully convince a person that they will greatly benefit if they use your product or service—that their life or business will be improved in some way, and that the gains will far outweigh the outlay of money and/or time and energy. You can prove your case with testimonials, facts, physical demonstrations, guarantees, pictures and references. The most powerful amongst these, however, is **the testimonial.**

And since what others say about you is many, many times more effective than what you say about yourself, <u>testimonials</u> are the key to creating successful copy that leads to people taking action. Including testimonials helps customers to do a cost/benefit analysis of your product in a more favorable light for you. This is because testimonials increase the credibility of your product and small business. They can transform potential scepticism and mistrust into advocacy, making people more confident to deal with your company.

Testimonials therefore = increased sales

Remember in the Business of Getting Results, it's <u>Not</u> about you—It's about Your Customer

There is a limit as to what you can say about yourself and your product without sounding egotistical. However, when someone else says complimentary things about your product, it acts as a very positive review. As a result, sales to prospects who've heard testimonials about you, are easier to make and, very importantly, more likely to be on your terms.

At *lead creation,* we know a lot about gaining testimonials because as a part of our marketing service, we help our clients find advocates amongst their own client base. We also provide a 'how to guide' to help our clients get great testimonials and how to record or video them. Then we show where and how to use these testimonials in their marketing to improve sales lead generation. You'll learn the most important aspects of that service later in this chapter.

Testimonials Don't Work... When You're Not Using Them!

More often than not, businesses have not yet effectively utilised testimonials for a number of reasons. When *lead creation* staff work with new clients, we commonly discover one of the following situations:

1. **The company has not collected many or any testimonials**

© www.leadcreation.com.au

2. The testimonials are just plain and boring, and are rarely used or not at all
3. They have written testimonials, but no video or audio ones – which are much more powerful
4. And worst of all – they have a lot of great testimonials or clients who are willing to give them, yet they are not being used!

So these small business owners and managers have been working hard and spending money to convey their marketing message to their prospects, while at the same time keeping their very best salesperson locked out of sight and out of mind! This is what you are doing when you leave testimonials unused. Clients who are willing to be advocates for your small business will convince potential customers better than any other kind of marketing as you only have a limited budget (it goes with the territory when you are in <u>small</u> business!). 'Word of mouth' recommendations spring from this, and this type of viral marketing is incredibly powerful and best of all, it's free! So how can you put your testimonials to good use?

If Your Company Provides Fantastic Service, *Flaunt It!*

It is difficult to overdo the use of testimonials in your marketing. You should use them a lot, and in as many different ways as possible. Why not record testimonials and put them onto a CD or Podcast to send out to prospects? Or you could film them and put them on a DVD or Vodcast. And of course put them on YouTube and on your website. The possibilities are endless.

These are all surprisingly cost-effective and simple ways of using testimonials. They work because people will listen to or watch far more than they would ever bother reading. It's also effective because people can't skim through a CD or a DVD in the same way they might a letter or email. This means that with these formats, you can effectively control the order in which the potential customer gets the testimonial or your pitch. And this makes this kind of marketing far more convincing and effective.

You can also make audio or video testimonials more interesting by dramatising them—use multiple voices, inflection, emphasis, music, sound effects and so on to make the content more interesting and engaging. CDs and DVDs of testimonials are also good because they can be passed on between people—and are still less likely to be thrown out than a letter because they have perceived value (though the perceived value of CDs is falling). People also will often watch them out of sheer curiosity, so here you have a valuable opportunity to present a good testimonial that sells your business effectively.

The Hierarchy of Credibility

As mentioned earlier, there is a hierarchy of credibility in how information is presented:

1. The most powerful is **you** (or your testimonial provider) meeting with the potential client <u>in person</u>
2. The second most powerful is **video**
3. Then it's **audio**
4. Finally the **written word** comes in last

Recorded testimonials therefore mean you always have an enthusiastic, persuasive salesman ready to talk to potential clients, twenty-four hours a day, and at the very moment that they're interested and want to find out more. Testimonials sell your product for you, and using them in your marketing is key to improving your small business marketing results.

Where to Start if you don't have *any* Testimonials?

If you don't have two testimonials to rub together, it's possible to gain some by offering a gift, or your product for free, in return for testimonials. However this is just to get the ball rolling. You should replace these testimonials with ones from happy customers who have paid for your service as soon as you have them.

If you have a long term product and no testimonials for the full thing, then you can get testimonials for everything else in the meantime. Focus on particular aspects of your service, rather than the total outcomes of using your product. Get testimonials that promote your customer service, the ease of the process, the convenience of your payment plan and so on. Supplement these with testimonials for the total outcome as soon as you have them.

You can also ask industry experts to review your offering and give testimonials. Testimonials from well known people or people associated with that market boost credibility for your service. Once you get these, use them! They will add credibility to your company and help overcome potential clients' initial lack of trust.

But no matter where you get testimonials from, make sure you get written permission to use them in your marketing. Explain the different ways you may use their testimonial and make sure the person is comfortable with this. They generally will be, but it is an important courtesy to extend.

Four Steps to a Glowing Testimonial

1. Do what you do better than anybody else: **exceed clients' expectations and turn them into advocates**

2. **Exchange your product or service in return for an honest written evaluation.** This strategy is mainly used when your product or service is new

3. **Include a questionnaire or survey form when the work is completed. To thank them for taking the time, you might offer them a small gift.** It should ask what you got right, what you got wrong, and how you can improve your product or service. This strategy also allows you to customise your product or service to your customers' needs. Remember: ask them to be honest, not kind. Have a "tick box" giving you permission to use what they say.

4. Everyone has clients who are advocates of what they do- people that are enthusiastic about your product or service and continue to do business with you. So **call your advocates and ask for a written or better yet, a video reference.** You'll be surprised by the number of people that agree.

How to get a Stellar Testimonial from Your Happy Client

It's important for you to be actively involved in the process of gaining testimonials because sometimes people will only give quite general or vague praise if they're not encouraged to say more. What is most convincing in a testimonial is detail and specifics. Also, some people are simply not naturally enthusiastic, even when happy. So to gain good testimonials from satisfied clients you can, and should ask questions about the specific things that you'd like your testimonials to promote.

In order to get good testimonials, ask your satisfied clients about:

- The specific benefits your product had for them
- What measurable results they saw
- How soon they saw measurable results
- Whether they've used other service providers or products like yours before and been unsatisfied
- Whether your product/services saved them time or money, and if so, how much?
- Whether they would recommend your services to their friends, family or colleagues?
- If they positively review you, ask what things in particular make them want to recommend you—Was it your friendly staff? Was it the efficiency with which you got back to them when they had questions? Was it the great advice you gave? Was it something else?

It's okay to coach people through their responses, because sometimes people will want to be an advocate for you but will just be too general in their testimonials to be of any real help. Specifics are more convincing, and so aim to get at these by targeting the questions you ask.

You should also ask testimonial givers if you can rewrite their testimonials, or edit sections. We all know that people 'umm and ahh' a bit when being questioned or filmed, and editing often helps to improve the clarity of the message. Send the edited version to the customer to make sure they're comfortable with the changes before you go ahead and use it in your marketing—ask them to respond by Reply email if they are happy with it.

5 Simple Ways to Improve the Believability & Effectiveness of Your Testimonials

1. **Proving Authenticity in Written Testimonials:** If you get a client's testimonial sent to you via letter, fax or email, you can document the date, time and sender and provide this wherever you use the testimonial. For an email you could do a screen capture (In windows by pressing the Print Screen button and then pasting it into Paint and saving the file) which shows the date and time you received it. This adds extra credibility with regards to the authenticity of the testimonial

2. **Address Buyer Objections:** Use your testimonials strategically to deal with the specific objections buyers would have. Here's an example from a computer business. In this situation the client's concerns would be:

   - **Is this a quality and reliable product?**
   - **Is the price better than what I've seen elsewhere?**
   - **Does the supplier provide ongoing support needs, and if so at what cost?**
   - **Is there a warranty or guarantee?**

3. **Layout:** Put a bold sub-head which is an abbreviation of the main points of the testimonial at the top of the testimonial. Put the testimonial itself in italics but not bolded. Include the full name and details of the testimonial provider on the last line. Even better, have a photograph of the person giving the testimonial and ask to use their signature. This way you can scan in the signature, adding to the credibility of the piece

4. **Information = Credibility:** In order to have believable testimonials, you should ideally have as much information about the person giving the testimonial as possible. A full name and details dramatically improves the believability of the testimonial in the

mind of the prospect. Ask to use the testimonial provider's full name, title, company name, suburb and state. Ask if you can use their company address as well (and this may be beneficial to get *them* more customers!). You might also provide dates for the period over which you worked with the client. You might even like to provide a picture of the testimonial giver (looking happy, of course) if they agree. The more information the better!

All these details help readers believe that the testimonial was spoken by a real person, someone like them who actually used your services and was satisfied with them. And this is the key to overcoming potential client scepticism about the benefits of using your company rather than your many competitors.

5. Don't be shy in using testimonials in your advertising, in your copy and on your website. **You can use subheads to introduce your testimonials, such as:**

    - **Here's what our clients say about us**
    - **Here are some real life examples**
    - **Real comments and case studies from satisfied clients**
    - **Read what others have to say**

Final Tip: Some clients just love your service and many will even have become friends. Within reason, they will say whatever you want them to say about the service or product you provide. But many just never get around to it because it takes time and is something out of the ordinary so is not easy.

The solution is to offer to write it for them to save them worrying about it—then they can edit it to reflect their views and their language and most will quickly email it back to you. Done and dusted!"

© www.leadcreation.com.au

Utilising the Power of Testimonials

If you have used testimonials before but are not sure how to utilise them further, here are a few ideas:

- Why not **decorate reception walls and offices** with framed testimonials and a picture of the testimonial giver, rather than simply hanging paintings and logos?
- Why not **print testimonials on your company stationery**, envelopes or packaging?
- If you have the name of your small business on a car or van, put some testimonials on it too
- Why not put **testimonials on your website, emails, newsletters or annual reviews**?
- Have an **FAQ** on your website where testimonials from clients answer all the questions and objections
- If a client gives a great testimonial, a way to make it even more convincing is to get permission to use their own company letterhead. You could then (with their express permission) print their testimonial under their letterhead and send it out as an endorsement of your company from their company
- Why waste <u>any</u> opportunity to use testimonials when, according to the American marketing guru Dan Kennedy, **"What others say about you and your product, service, or business is at least 1000% more convincing than what you say, even if you are 1000% more eloquent."**

Testimonials for *lead creation* are available on our website: http://www.leadcreation.com.au/testimonials. Feel free to visit and see what people are saying about us.

What Does *lead creation* do with Testimonials to Generate Sales Leads for our Clients?

We teach our clients how to gain and use valuable client testimonials. A key element of the **lead creation** marketing system is to have audio and video testimonials on our clients' online media such as their blog and website. We teach clients how to use written testimonials effectively on their website and in emails, faxes, newsletters, blogs, White Papers and in print advertisements. We also provide guidelines on how to set up video testimonials and we film and edit two of them for our clients. These are then displayed on their website to further establish expertise and the value of the services they provide. *You too can do all of these things for your own company, starting today!*

Finally, What Does a Good Testimonial Look Like?

Here is an example of a testimonial a *lead creation* client gave when we asked:

We Achieved a 32% Sales Growth in Australia thanks to *lead creation*

*"Like many businesses, we had a great product but not enough people knew about it. That's why we went to **lead creation**—and they had a huge impact on our business.*

*We worked with Toby Marshall and **lead creation** in mid 2008 when the GFC was starting and even during this appalling market managed to achieve a sales growth of 32%. We've had even better results in our much bigger UK market.*

*The **lead creation** strategies are simple but effective for businesses with a good product who just need more prospects to hear about it. And the best part was, I didn't have to go on the road and do any hard selling! The **lead creation** system really works to bring in qualified leads for my company."*

Paul Resnik
(Author and consultant to the Financial Advisory industry in Australia and globally)

We've used our testimonials in this book, on our website, in emails we've sent out, in our White Papers, on product brochures and in many other locations. Once you've got a great testimonial, don't be afraid to use it! **Reap the benefits by utilising testimonials that sell your business for you.** *Why Wait?*

Chapter 13: Interns—The Untapped Resource that Could Be Your Secret Weapon

Improve Your Profitability & Efficiency with Interns

We live in a constantly changing technological environment—from software, to the internet and social networking. The opportunities for small businesses are growing every day, as are the challenges. And who better to help you take advantage of these than student interns, a labor force made up of young people who are great at working with the internet and software.

So much of modern marketing involves technology, and it's what young people have grown up with and what they know—internet marketing is second nature. At *lead creation* we have tried and tested the use of unpaid interns. We currently have eighteen enthusiastic work-experience students and interns (aged from fifteen to twenty-five) and have mentored, managed and trained them into highly skilled and professional workers. To date we have helped over forty of them find great jobs when they graduate.

Don't Make them get Coffee—Give Them Work!

To start with, give them specific, narrow jobs and give them full responsibility to implement their ideas. Week by week, you'll see their skills improve through on the job learning and mentoring. When you work alongside interns, you discover what they're really good at, and where they'll be able to help your business. An intern may start in one position but discover along the way that their passion is really for a different aspect of your business. Be flexible, and you'll benefit from their enthusiasm to learn and their dedication to work.

If, however, you only send your interns to do Joe jobs like get the coffee or the lunches, or sort through the mail, or stuff envelopes, they are likely to get bored and become unproductive. Let them have a little bit of responsibility and more often than not you'll be surprised how hard they're willing to work. They're interning to get experience to put on their résumé, to gain a good reference, and to learn important work skills. It doesn't really make sense that they'd put in all the effort to apply for an internship which they're only going to slack off in. So let them take some of the work off your shoulders.

It's a Win-Win Situation

Not only will it save your company money, but it also creates an opportunity for motivated young people looking to get experience in the corporate world while they are still at uni. It's an extremely rewarding experience, for both parties if set up properly.

And it also has the following benefit—it's cost effective for you. Using interns will allow you to drop your charge-out rates and offer your services at a more competitive price. Interns are a low-cost and high-return option for small professional businesses willing to put in the proper energy and time into hiring, mentoring and developing the skills of their young interns.

Find Only the Very Best & Dedicated Interns

In our business *lead creation*, we frequently hire unpaid interns to take on specific and strategic learning roles that are related to their studies.

This is a great opportunity for the intern to gain experience in the corporate world and also to develop expertise in a field they're interested in entering when they graduate.

Our Interns:
- are typically undergraduate university students with a year or more left to complete for their degrees
- are allowed a very flexible schedule—they work for us on days that suit them, working around their university and part-time job commitments
- are allowed to work a day or two from home per week if this better suits to them (many live in the outer suburbs)
- the very best of them are hired to work with us after their unpaid period of twenty-five days has been completed
- for the ones that don't stay on with us, we are happy to write references for and to act as referees for when they apply for new jobs
- we set up LinkedIn profiles and blogs for each intern—and our clients have started to write recommendations on their profiles for the work they've done. This is a great leg up when they are applying for jobs in the future! Testimonials for real work while still a student—priceless!

We advertise our internship roles on job boards like Seek and Monster, and communicate the limits and benefits very clearly. Due to our efforts to make our internship roles appealing to undergraduates, we consistently have a large number of applicants applying for these positions. We then have the opportunity to be selective with whom we interview and can assure that we hire only the very best candidates—good students that also fit our jobs so both sides benefit.

To ensure this, we screen cover letters and résumés and then conduct phone interviews with the standouts. If the phone interview is strong, we ask for two work (not academic) references and call to ask questions about the potential intern (all of our interns must have had jobs, even if only in a bar). If these two reference checks go well, we will then call the candidate in for a face-to-face interview with our Human Resources staff. We will generally interview three or four interns for every position we are hiring for so that we can be sure we hire the very best candidate—the one who performed best across the board. Before the approximately thirty to forty minute interview, we also conduct a spelling and grammar test with our potential interns. We assess their punctuality, presentation and performance in the interview and from there we make a decision as to whether this is the right person for the role.

As you can see, we conduct a very detailed assessment before we choose to hire any interns to work in our business. This is so we can be assured we're getting the best person for the job and also so that the intern knows we are serious about how and who we hire. The intern will understand that we set a high professional standard and so work to maintain this standard during their time with us.

How to Ensure Your Interns Stay the Duration

In order to ensure your intern doesn't give up halfway through, there are a number of things you should do:

- Emphasise the fact that the internship is valuable work experience that they can put on their résumé
- Explain how they will develop expertise in their chosen internship role
- Offer them good on-the-job training, learning resources, and mentoring from senior staff

- Communicate effectively with them. Remember that at first it's overwhelming for them—it's probably their first experience in "A Real Job" and so is usually a steep learning curve
- Put them on specific projects and give them full responsibility to act on them
- Check with their progress, offer feedback and encouragement
- Don't talk down to them or hide them away from clients
- Be patient with them in the beginning. Just remember that they've never done this before
- Treat them just as you would any other member of your staff
- Involve them in company get-togethers, events, drinks, birthday celebrations—let them be a part of your company culture
- Go to lunch with them or encourage your staff to all go out to lunch together (interns included)
- Assign them a mentor within your company who will check on the intern and make sure they're happy and focused
- Make sure you're approachable to them to discuss any issues they're having or to query any work they don't understand
- Explain concepts that are important for your business to them. Remember that it's not innate knowledge to them. They haven't worked in the field before—in fact, most of them have never worked in an office.

How to Manage Your Interns so They're Happy & Productive

If you're seriously considering hiring an intern, here are some tips on how to manage your new recruit. Following these will ensure both parties to get the most out of this partnership.

1. Be flexible. Depending on the individual intern, where they live and their university timetable, it may be easier for them to work full or part days from home. You should generally have your intern do a minimum of two days a week or they will become unfocused and your small business won't get the value. It may also be possible for them to work longer hours during university holidays and so it's helpful to both of you if you can arrange to accommodate this.

2. As most interns have experience in either the Retail or Hospitality industries, training on commencement is extremely important, as is ongoing learning. The more time you spend mentoring your intern, the more valuable they will become.

3. As the intern is not in the office every day, the work needs to be project driven and not overly time critical. If the work is urgent, it must be capable of being transferred to someone else fairly quickly. It must also be interesting work as the intern will then feel like they are making a valuable contribution to the business.

4. Getting your intern to do some general administrative duties is fine so long as the intern knows when they need to be completed by. And that there is not too much of it.

5. The intern needs to know where your business is heading to feel part of it. Get them involved as that really increases their level of enthusiasm.

6. There needs to be clear objectives, goals and expectations set with 'SMART' timeframes (i.e. Specific, Measurable, Achievable, Realistic and Timely).

7. Feedback needs to take place on a regular basis, both positive and constructive to improve skills and increase their experience.

8. Interns like responsibility, but let them prove that they can handle it first.

9. Be flexible around exam time as it is a very stressful time and they may require a little more time off to study. (This was written by one of our HR interns!)

10. We recommend informal performance reviews with your intern to occasionally go through the company and employee's objectives.

Questions You (or a Mentor) Can Ask Your Intern

Once you've got your intern working on projects, it's easy to begin thinking of them as just another member of the team. It's helpful however to check in with them from time to time to make sure that they're happy and that they feel like they're on track. You, or a senior staff member you've assigned to mentor them, can ask an intern some of these questions from time to time. Showing care and concern for your intern goes a long way to making them feel appreciated and motivated to continue putting in their best efforts. It also helps your office run more smoothly and gives interns a chance to bring up any issues they are having before they get out of hand.

You, or a mentor, could ask your intern:

- What were your first impressions of your internship at this business?
- How do you feel about working here?
- Do you need more support regarding your duties?
- Is there anything that you're not happy about?
- What have you learnt so far?
- What do you want to learn more about?
- What did you expect coming into this internship?
- Were your expectations matched/not matched?
- What has been your best experience so far?
- What was your worst experience?
- Is there anything you expected to learn or do here that isn't happening?
- Do you have any questions for me?

Take the time to listen to their answers and talk through any issues or queries they may have. This will ensure your intern feels they are getting the proper support in their role and also that there is someone in the company who they can talk to if they're unsure about anything. This helps ensure they stay for the duration of their internship and don't give up half way through because they feel like they don't know what they're doing or what the heck you want.

When it's Time for an Intern to Leave...

Unfortunately, most small businesses won't be able to offer every intern the chance to stay on working for them for any number of reasons. However, this is a good opportunity to learn from their experience in order to improve your internship process. When an intern (or any staff member) leaves your company, it can often be beneficial to conduct an

Exit Interview to find out how they felt during their time at your company and any areas of your staff culture or work philosophy that could use improvement. Ask questions about:

- whether they were satisfied with the kind of tasks they were asked to do
- what else they would have liked to learn
- whether they would recommend your company as a place for their friends to work or intern (why/why not?)
- If they were unhappy or unsatisfied with anything at work
- How any problems or issues they had could have been better addressed
- What they think was the main benefit they received from working with you
- How the internship process could be improved in any way
- Whether they felt like a valued member of your business
- Whether they got constructive feedback for their work
- Whether their jobs were clearly defined and explained to them
- Whether they received enough training

From the feedback you receive from your exiting staff and interns, you can learn how to make your small business a better and more productive place to work. You can also constructively use this feedback to change your internship hiring and management processes to ensure that these young people feel happy, productive, and on track throughout their time with you.

Toby Marshall, Director of *lead creation*, on What it's *Really* like Working with Interns

"In 2008 I was wondering how to make my services more appealing to clients. How could I make my services more affordable? This caused me to ask a question to my staff that changed everything.

I said, 'We've regularly had work experience students come join us from the US and Germany, but could we find some interns from Oz to work for us?' There was a long pause but then Sean my HR associate replied, 'Why not? We'd just apply the same rigorous process when hiring interns as we would when hiring paid staff and then we'd be sure we're getting the right people.'

So from then on, I began hiring interns to work in my business. We now have nineteen marketing and IT interns working with us, six of whom are now paid staff. This has meant that we've been able to drop our rates, and this has helped us gain more business during the GFC. But it's meant so much more than that as well. The energy of these talented young people is a great energiser for old guys like me. These really are enthusiastic, young professionals doing what young people do best—technology and innovation.

We posted ads for unpaid internships and a surprising number applied – I discovered that there were a lot of talented students looking for corporate experience while still at uni. We initially spent nine months creating training processes and systems to make this large team productive. During their time with us, we mentor our interns into highly skilled and professional workers. The best of them go onto full salaries with us, and others we've helped find great jobs afterwards. It's been great for their careers to gain REAL experience.

Interns are excited to work and learn, and its fun to have them around. It brings life into the office. I'd recommend hiring an intern to any professional business willing to do it right. It's a low-cost and high-return option for small professional businesses."

Toby Marshall, June 2009

© www.leadcreation.com.au

For more information on generating qualified leads, getting more customers, making more sales & creating an automated marketing system:

Visit us soon at:

www.leadcreation.com.au

- Access free video guides
- Download free marketing reports and articles
- Learn more about our company and dynamic team
- Read more client testimonials
- Find out about the work we do for clients

For more information, read our tweets:

www.leadcreation.com.au/about/twitter-feed

http://twitter.com/Toby_Marshall

Watch our informative how to videos on:

www.youtube.com/leadcreation

Visit our blogs at:

www.smallbusinessleads.com.au

& www.tobymarshall.com

And find us on LinkedIn and Facebook by searching 'lead creation' or 'Toby Marshall'

More Praise for Toby Marshall!

"If you are a small business needing to get smarter about your marketing you need to speak with Toby. His creative, simple ideas on how to get known by your niche via the use of LinkedIn are superb. If you need to develop more leads and get more sales you owe it to yourself to have a conversation with Toby."

Hugh Gyton
Speaker, Author & Conversation Skills Coach

"Toby's valuable seminar on why and how to use LinkedIn is informative whilst entertaining. Toby thinks very strategically about social networking and how it fits into a broader marketing strategy."

James Brenan,
Financial Adviser, Fairchild Financial Services

"Toby is changing the way CEOS think. His work is creating a fundamental shift in the culture of some corporate Thought Leaders."

Matt Church,
CEO of Thought Leaders

"I recently attended a workshop by Toby Marshall and was highly impressed! Brilliant information. Now I really have an idea how things work, what to do, what not to do. Am truly grateful that Toby shared his expertise so generously."

Maja Meschitschek,
Independent Telecommunications Professional

"I attended one of Toby's excellent business development seminars. I came away with several new ideas and have already put two of them into practice. His generosity in sharing info around lead generation & marketing to small-medium professional service firms (such as my own) is awe inspiring. My business should definitely grow because of Toby!"

Julie Garland McLellan,
CEO at Corporate Governance and Board Consultant

© www.leadcreation.com.au

"Have had the opportunity to hear Toby speak both in the US and Canada. Toby is insightful and engaging and his unique point of view forces even seasoned veterans to rethink the way they do their jobs."

Judy Tilmont,
Executive Recruiter, Driggers & Blackwell Personnel

"Toby is a professional Manager and Marketer. He is innovative and forward looking and I value his insights into Consulting and Business Generation. We initially shared business premises and resources—a true test of a trusting relationship—and have subsequently shared insights into our businesses."

Geoff & Isobel Berry
Managing Directors, The Berry Group

"I first worked with Toby in 1989. Since that initial encounter he has always inspired as a true 'why can't it be done' style of entrepreneurial ideas guy. Having vision and determination he is always ahead of the pack when it comes to leading edge ideas that will change the way we think about the world and ultimately about how we interact with it."

Ian Hamilton,
Managing Director, Carroll Consulting Group

"Toby Marshall is one of a kind. Where others zig he zags. He is a creative thinker who is able to provide a unique service and strong track record of delivery. He is a pioneer in an industry reluctant to change."

Jason Elias
Owner Elias Recruitment

"When Toby speaks, people listen. His passion and commitment in all areas of his business are always evident when he is on the stage. His enthusiasm is contagious, he is a master networker and I thoroughly enjoy watching Toby speak."

Neen James,
Owner Need James Communications

"Toby is visionary and energising. Working with Toby as a supplier is exhilarating; working with Toby as a client is nothing but rewarding. We are constantly impressed by his insights and ability to solve the seemingly intractable problems clients present him with. If Toby believes in your business, he will do all he can to make it a success."

Anna Savage,
Managing Account Director at Loud Mouth PR

"Attended a workshop presented by Toby and was very impressed with the level of understanding and knowledge regarding social media, as well as the many creative ideas for promotion of small businesses that were presented. I am definitely interested in attending future workshops to further increase my knowledge, and improve the results of my business marketing."

Benjamin Townsend
Owner of Benjamin Townsend Photography

"Toby's insights into marketing and social media are tremendous. His advice is highly practical. Anyone and everyone can put it to use immediately."

Rosemary Gillespie
Tender & Proposal Writer at Proof Communications

"Toby is Australia's LinkedIn marketing expert. Most people just have LinkedIn, Some people use LinkedIn, but Toby GETS LinkedIn and it's power as a marketing tool. I've seen his passion to help professional service people unlock the real potential in Linked In. So if you want to know how to turn your connections into leads, I'd chat with Toby."

Ashton Bishop,
General Manager of ThinkCentric Group

© www.leadcreation.com.au